Charlene White

No Place Like Home

RENEGADE BOOKS

First published in Great Britain in 2024 by Renegade Books
An imprint of John Murray Press

This paperback edition published in 2025

1

A CIP catalogue record for this title is available from the British Library.

Paperback ISBN 978-0-349-70366-4

Typeset in Berling by M Rules

Printed and bound in Great Britain by Clays Ltd, Elcograf S.p.A.

John Murray policy is to use papers that are natural, renewable and recyclable
products and made from wood grown in sustainable forests. The logging and
manufacturing processes are expected to conform to the environmental
regulations of the country of origin.

Carmelite House
50 Victoria Embankment
London EC4Y 0DZ

www.dialoguebooks.co.uk

John Murray Press, part of Hodder & Stoughton Limited
An Hachette UK company

The authorised representative in the EEA is Hachette Ireland,
8 Castlecourt Centre, Dublin 15, D15 XTP3, Ireland (email: info@hbgi.ie)

Award-winning journalist and broadcaster, **Charlene White** is an ITV News presenter, a BAFTA-nominated and Royal Television Society-winning *Loose Women* host and a pioneer at the forefront of news broadcasting.

Charlene is a columnist for the *i* paper, has previously worked as a writer for the *New York Post*, and presented for BBC Radio 1 and 1Xtra, BBC News Channel, BBC Five Live and BBC Three. She co-hosted, alongside Sir Trevor McDonald, the notable documentary *Has George Floyd Changed Britain?*, exploring the impact George Floyd's death had on people living in the UK, and hosted her own prime-time ITV documentary, *Empire's Child*, looking at where her family sits in the British Empire. Charlene took part in the twenty-second series of *I'm A Celebrity ... Get Me Out of Here!* and embarked on the *Loose Women Live* regional tour.

Charlene uses her platform to educate children about race and racism, mentor aspiring journalists and work alongside various organisations to achieve better representation of women and minorities in the industry, winning a Royal Television Society award for Best Children's programme explaining racism and Black Lives Matter to children. *No Place Like Home* is Charlene's debut work of non-fiction.

Contents

Introduction

I shall return again; I shall return
To laugh and love and watch with wonder-eyes
At golden noon the forest fires burn,
Wafting their blue-black smoke to sapphire skies.
I shall return to loiter by the streams
That bathe the brown blades of the bending grasses,
And realize once more my thousand dreams
Of waters rushing down the mountain passes.
I shall return to hear the fiddle and fife
Of village dances, dear delicious tunes
That stir the hidden depths of native life,
Stray melodies of dim remembered runes.
I shall return, I shall return again,
To ease my mind of long, long years of pain.

'I Shall Return', CLAUDE MCKAY, 1922

Read this poem above a couple of times and see if it elicits any kind of reaction. No? Well, me neither the first time I read it. It just seemed like a normal, you know, poem. Beautiful? Yes.

Emotive? Absolutely. But nothing particularly special, to be honest. However, what I'd like you to do is keep the poem at the back of your mind for a bit, then reread it when you get to the end of this introduction. Then read it again when you get to the end of this book and see how you feel. See if the words take on extra resonance. It took me a beat to get it – well, it took me about five days of filming in Jamaica for my ITV documentary *Empire's Child* (made by Doc Hearts) to finally understand and *feel* its words.

In no way am I suggesting you hop on a flight to a far-flung destination, but what I'm hoping is that through the stories I tell in this book, this poem makes you think about where 'home' sits in the story of your life. That it makes you reflect on where or what you may want to return to, as the poem suggests. When the penny finally dropped with me, it was a visceral and unexpected reaction that suddenly bubbled to the surface and overflowed uncontrollably. It was primal. It felt like I wasn't in control of my body. It wasn't as if the tears started coming slowly, it was as though years of pent-up immigrant emotions that had been building like a pressure cooker in my heart had suddenly burst. And with it came tears that overflowed. It was like I'd lost control of my legs. My *entire* body was hit by this juggernaut of emotions. My legs buckled, and I was bent over and groaning in pain; not physical – emotional. With that came the dripping of my tears onto the red dirt of the land of my ancestor's birth. My heart was hurt, sad, joyful and at peace, all in one fell swoop. For me, it was weird and unexpected.

But if you get even half of that, it's a connection that may sit with you for a while.

A historian was explaining the importance of this location to the history of the maternal side of my family; although I have distant relatives who still live in the area, I wasn't aware of the origins of the connection, or just how far back it went. When I got out of the car, I could hear the familiar sound of reggae blaring out of someone's sound system down the road, the sound of chickens housed in the coop in the garden of a house behind me. It was early afternoon after a journey which had seemed to take hours as the car weaved its way along the roads that twirled themselves round and round the hills in the searing heat of the day, as the driver tried to avoid the plentiful potholes that peppered the tarmac almost continuously. When we arrived and slid the door of the car open, what I wanted was the breath in fresh air that could bring some relief from the exhaustion and the passing car sickness – what I got instead was a slap in the face from the intensity of the heat that was beating down at the top of that hill. There was to be no relief from the heat that day, which made the bubbling emotions of the day become ever-more magnified.

We'd spent the day talking to various historians about my family's connection to the slave trade, the aim being to find out more about the mixed heritage of my great-great-great-grandfather William Stanbury. That day we'd discovered that he was included on a list of enslaved people who were owned by John Stanbury – a white slave owner. The historian had concluded that John had listed his own children as property that he owned: making John my great-great-great-great-grandfather. As to whether William was a son he ever acknowledged we were never able to ascertain, so it had been an eye-opening but also frustrating day.

No one would tell me *why* we were on the top of that mountain; the producers kept repeating that my curiosity about the puzzle would soon be satiated. I looked out towards the valleys that were created by the swooping hill ahead. Lush green produce lay ahead as far as you could see. And it was a beautiful as you can imagine. I was then told to walk down the hill where another historian would join us to talk me through why we were on that hill.

She gestured towards a stretch of lush green land behind me, and explained that somewhere in there was the first piece of land my family ever owned when they became free. The name of that couple was Andrew and Elsey Pusey; they were enslaved people in Jamaica in the 1790s and became two of the first freed when slavery was abolished in 1834. Through the slave owner allowing them to buy a piece of land to call their own, they were able to grow fruit and vegetables to sell at the local market. That in turn put in motion a series of events which would lead to my grandfather, in the 1970s, upping sticks and moving to the UK, and my parents settling in the country of my birth. It was almost like a butterfly effect: the wings of my ancestors back in the 1830s caused a ripple effect that was still being felt today. To finally find out the catalyst responsible for the history of my family was quite something. And that's when I glanced down at the poem again and its symbolism made sense. *I* had returned.

I've always felt like a sum of many parts. I'm British, I was born here, and I've lived here my entire life. But I'm also Jamaican. The food, traditions, culture, language and personality traits of my ancestors are integral to who I am. But all those things are also true of the British side of me. It's been a learning curve. I remember being at a birthday Sunday lunch at a mate's house when I was in my early twenties. Her mum brought all the food to the table and sat down, and everyone started eating. I was aghast. I said to her mum that she'd forgotten to bring the rice to the table. Everyone looked at me confused, and my friend Chantal explained that English Sunday dinner doesn't include rice – it blew my mind, folks. BLEW MY MIND! By that point I'd spent almost twenty years of my life having rice with my dinner every Sunday (for we Jamaicans, rice is very much a staple). I genuinely thought that's what everyone did!

So, what home feels and looks like for me can be varied and beautiful and full of contradictions. London is my home, England is my home, Britain is my home, Jamaica is my home, the Caribbean is my home. My DNA shows that West Africa is also historically my home. But where among these myriad coordinates on a world map is the place that's home in my heart? It's a difficult one really. When your lineage is spread out across three continents, trying to navigate in your mind to the location that fills every part of your being with a sense of stillness, with a hint of belonging, and a side of peace can be a tough one. It's one that I still struggle with, to be honest. I often find that I feel like a square peg trying to force myself into a round hole. Only parts of it fit, and the rest is left out. There are still so many instances where I have to explain why my hair is different, or why I still have to put sunblock on ('You burn, really?!'), it can be tiring. It's moments like that that make you wonder if home can really be the place where you find yourself constantly having to explain parts of yourself.

Through the process of writing this book, I spoke to lots of people about how they view the world in terms of home. And with each interview I would gain even more clarity, and yet still be more confused, because each person saw it very differently.

I've always felt incredibly lucky to have been born and raised in London. It's where we're raising our children. Just under half of the people who live here identify as an ethnic minority[1] and its sights, smells and sounds are very much a reflection of that. Walk through parts of London and you could be transported to a place in the world that you'd never been fortunate to set foot in before. And yet here, you can. It's a bus, Tube, train or walk away. Save for a few stints working abroad, and elsewhere in the UK, I've lived in London my whole life. So, does that make it home?

On the other side of the coin, I have friends who packed up their lives and headed to London in their twenties, lured by the city of opportunity, hoping to make their mark in the world. For those who've spent over half their lives living here, does London feel like home? Or are they, like me, slightly conflicted over exactly what home means? For many of them it means jumping on a train and walking through their family's front door to the smell of their mum's cooking, the sound of their dad watching footy too loudly in the living room and their siblings mostly ignoring them but secretly excited to see them. For others it could be jewellery handed down from grandma, a scarf that smells like mum, notes left in a book by their dad, or just stepping off a plane and smelling the familiar air of where you grew up.

I grew up in Lewisham in south-east London, an area

which, according to the latest census, is the local authority with the highest proportion of people identifying as Black. Not a surprise since, at times, it felt like I lived in a Jamaican household in a corner of London that was quintessentially Caribbean. It was a beautiful place to be raised. At home there was me, my younger brother Joshua and sister Carina, the textbook middle-child. And, of course, my mum and dad, Dorrett and Denniston. Memories can sometimes be skewed over time, I know that, but I remember it as a house that was never truly quiet: there was always one of my parent's friends popping in unannounced if they were driving by (pre-mobile phones, obviously), or one of my many aunts and uncles, usually with a couple of cousins in tow. Our house was the centre for so many people, and we all loved it that way.

It was sold in my mid-twenties when we became a blended stepfamily. So as a fully fledged, card-carrying, bill-paying grown-up, any cravings I've had for 'going home' have never been satiated. I've always been slightly jealous of people who return to their old bedrooms at Christmas, and I've often wondered what it might have been like to run 'back home' when my heart had been broken by boys masquerading as men, or when the heaviness of grown-up life became too much. Or to have my kids experience sleeping over in my old bedroom, complete with posters of RnB bands from a bygone era – Jodeci, Take That, Ultimate Kaos – the windows slightly stained by the nicotine of friends sneakily smoking out of my window.

Maybe I'd been desperately trying to find home when I started the journey of looking into my family history. The weight of what I might find to complete the puzzle was sitting very heavily on my shoulders when I arrived in Jamaica in the summer of 2021. As soon as I stepped off the plane, I breathed in that Jamaican air for the first time in three years, and against my better judgement I could just feel the British stiff-upper-lip attitude I'd flown over with slowly but surely ebbing away. I'd left London with the attitude that whatever I found wasn't going to move me; in fact, I didn't *want* it to move me. History is history, right? Why should it have any impact on my present? But what I know now is just how wrong, infantile and ill-judged that was. What I hadn't realised, as the plane started its ascent from Gatwick, was that sometimes you have no control over the way your body can react to things: sometimes your body processes it first, while your brain plays catch-up.

Like many immigrants, my family is transient. And like many Jamaican families, I'm the descendant of 450 years of enslaved people, meaning that Britain has been part of my make-up for quite some time; even though to many, my darker skin means that I'm anything but. So perhaps that's why 'home' can be so difficult to quantify for me and so many others. When your family's been moved from pillar to post and has started from scratch so many times, it can be hard to know where you belong. It can be hard to pinpoint the place where, when its smells fill your lungs, when your feet touch its soil, when its sounds fill your ears, when your eyes widen with recognition of its scenery . . . it immediately feels like home.

The journey to find my roots and figure out where I came from was sparked by my Aunty Eleanor, upon the death of her dad, my grandad Byron. Once he was gone, she lost any answers to her questions about our family history. It's not to say that something was missing from her life, it's just that she wanted more of an understanding of where she came from. I guess she – like me – just wanted to feel complete. To feel whole. If there's one thing that I would constantly tell people, it is to ask those questions of your elders while they're still here, because once they've gone the answers could be gone for ever.

That was something that never crossed my mind in my twenties. I just wasn't really that bothered about feeling whole, I was too busy partying hard and enjoying life. The yearning didn't turn up in my thirties either. But then I had kids and reached my forties. And I suppose I felt a bit discombobulated. I was a mother learning to mother without a mother, and I felt a bit out of sorts. Unfinished, somehow. I've definitely taken a lot of my mum's mothering traits. I often hear her as I speak her words when I'm telling the kids off, or when I'm praising them for conquering a task. 'Ooh nah earr muss feel' was one of her favourites [Translation: 'If you don't hear you will feel.' Which basically means if you don't do as you are told you're likely to get reprimanded]. Another favourite, 'Yuh nah tek up a book from maarning?' [Translation: 'Have you done any schoolwork today?']. Oh, and this one I heard frequently due to my always-inquisitive mind: 'Yuh fi come outta big people business' [Translation: 'This is an adult conversation']. I may not repeat them verbatim to my kids, but the sentiment is basically the same.

I often wonder if my mum got those words and phrases from her mum and dad, and did my grandparents get them from their parents? What did they want to keep from their lives growing up in the Caribbean and pass on to their children, and what did they want to leave behind? What parenting and life traits did they pick up when they moved to Britain, and did they feel any less Jamaican being here? I'll just never know because I didn't bother asking my grandparents or my mum when they were alive.

I do often wonder if those who move away from the country of their birth make a conscious decision to pick and choose which elements of their life they take with them, and which they are happy to leave behind. I think I had a very Caribbean upbringing, very strict in parts, very focused on education, and always keeping us on a very short lead. My parents were also very wary of eating anywhere other than the houses of people they knew personally, just in case their kitchen was unsanitary or their hygiene standards were questionable. It took them a really long time to mellow out and let me eat at friends' houses. That was after they had mellowed and allowed me to go to friends' houses in the first place. Both of these scenarios are peak Jamaican in terms of the way my mum and dad handled and instilled discipline.

But I do understand that they were feeling their way in terms of how to parent in their second home. They had been raised with one kind of parenting in Jamaica, another with Jamaican parents in London, and were now trying to figure out their own version of that scenario. My dad had clearly figured it out once my younger brother reached his teens, since he was basically allowed to do anything. I might as well have been locked up for my entire teens compared to the freedom that child enjoyed.

My mum and her siblings all moved to Britain – my aunt

arrived first aged eleven and the others joined them in the years that followed. My dad moved here in his late teens. But so many of their generation immediately moved back to Jamaica once they reached retirement age, despite so many of them spending more than half their lives in Britain. To them, time changed nothing. Home was always Jamaica, no matter how many years were spent here. Which is true of many immigrants who move to the UK – irrespective of their original country of birth. I spoke to my Uncle Errol about it for the documentary. This is a man who moved to London in his early teens and moved back to Jamaica in his sixties. He put it more far more eloquently and succinctly than I ever could: 'Charlene, Jamaica is the land of my heart. Britain was the land of opportunity.'

When he said that it really hit me, you know? We were sat on a wall overlooking the port in Jamaica's capital, Kingston. We hadn't seen each other for three years, since the last time I was in Jamaica, so we were perched on this wall catching up. The country was still taking tentative steps out of the Covid-19 pandemic so the city was still really quiet. It felt at times like we were the only people in the port that day, and it was very different to the Kingston I had visited over the years. What hadn't changed was my uncle; moving 'back home' made him seem younger somehow. His skin was glowing, his smile seemed brighter, he seemed more statuesque than before. Since returning, he definitely appeared more at peace; there was a stillness about him.

Talking to my uncle at the port that day may well have been the point when I started questioning where home is supposed to be for me. Can a country still be seen as the land of opportunity if you're born here? I'm not quite sure. But before we even get to that, I've got to figure out what home actually means. It's by no means a simple dictionary definition; that's too basic.

Home: a noun meaning the place where one lives permanently, especially as a member of a family or household.

As I said, the *literal* definition is too basic. It goes far deeper than that.

Over the years I'd just taken it for granted that of course my dad and my uncle were going to move back to Jamaica in retirement. I don't remember a time in my life when that *wasn't* the plan. They talked about it enough when I was a kid, and had been saving incessantly for years to be able to achieve that dream.

But that was *their* home. So where was mine? I remember snippets of just about every family trip to Jamaica. I remember my grandad buying a goat when we arrived one year when I was seven years old. I think I was even with him when the seller brought it to the house. My grandad spent weeks fattening up this goat. I think I may have even helped him feed it; I'm not sure I was entirely certain why there was a random goat tied to the tree in my grandad's front garden. But I genuinely think I decided to just roll with it.

I remember very clearly when D-day arrived: literally 'Death-Day'. The day before my mum's birthday was when the penny dropped: they were going to kill it. I remember my mum shutting me in the house and closing the curtains, without really properly explaining what was happening. But

I, with the aforementioned inquisitive mind, waited for her to leave the room, then went straight to the curtains and cracked them open wide enough so that I could see, but not wide enough that the grown-ups outside could spot what I had achieved. And I watched the whole thing unfold, fascinated.

As an adult I do realise why they wanted to hide it from me. They wanted me to love the land of their birth, their home, and understand my roots. What they didn't want is for me to be traumatised by watching a goat's head being hacked off, and associate Jamaica with that trauma for ever. But in the end, it was my mum, and not me, who had an everlasting reaction to events that afternoon. She became a semi-vegetarian that year. I, on the other hand, thought the curry goat was absolutely delicious.

Having taken my kids to Jamaica a couple of times I can completely understand why my parents wouldn't want their children to associate the country of their birth with any negative connotations. My Aunty Annette in Jamaica raises chicks and sells the chicken, plucked and ready to cook, once they're fully grown. When I was there last there, she had a new batch of chicks which both my children (Alfie, aged six; Florence, aged four) were obsessed with. I explained in very careful terms what lay in the chicken's future, but I wouldn't expose them to the last few minutes of the birds' lives, just in case that's what they would always associate Jamaica with. I want them to feel connected to it like I do, and I want them to know, understand and respect their roots. Although, saying that, Florence is more like me personality-wise, and would more than likely find it fascinating rather than grotesque.

With all the years I've spent toing and froing between

Jamaica and Britain both as a child and adult, I often wonder if I should feel even more Jamaican – in a similar way to my parents? The fact is, my blood is Jamaican. I may have been born in Greenwich, London, and have a British passport but I have two Jamaican parents. Every inch of the blood flowing through my veins is Jamaican so should I really consider my home to be anywhere else? Again, it comes down to the definition of home. But the spanner in the works, of course, is that my DNA shows that my bloodline is not that of the Awaraks (the indigenous population of Jamaica). It lies further afield.

I had my DNA tested for the TV programme and there was a strong presence in Nigeria, the connection obviously being the Transatlantic Slave Trade. This nugget of information will come with a level of annoyance from my Ghanaian friends who are absolutely convinced that I belong to them. Britain's lucrative slave trade is well documented, and my DNA shows that my ancestors were native to the west of Africa but were transported alongside an estimated 12.5 million men, women, and children in ships to the Caribbean and the United States as part of a slave trade that killed countless people who were forced into a life of servitude to line the pockets of those who cared little for people whose skin was darker than theirs. Around 12 per cent of those who started the voyage didn't survive.

So, my DNA markers were not hugely surprising. For most Jamaicans their ancestry leads them to faraway places they've only ever seen on TV and read about in books. Very few have had the chance to walk the land from which they came, their ground zero when it comes to their home. The villages and towns from which my ancestors were dragged, however, will never be known. The British didn't care to keep those kinds of records, because Black enslaved bodies did not warrant that sort of attention to detail.

When my dad visited the Gambia a few years ago to stay with friends, he returned and regaled us with stories of the sense of belonging he experienced from the moment he arrived. On more than one occasion when he was walking around, Gambians thought he was a local, and when he visited Kunte Kinteh Island, one of the slave ports, he had the same visceral feeling that I described at the start of this introduction. My dad isn't an overtly emotional man, we're very similar in that way, so for him to say that he suddenly felt a connection really is something.

This is a place he visited for the first time in his sixties, in a country he'd never set foot in before, but a land in which his ancestors had once roamed freely, until that freedom was so brutally ended. It does, then, beg the question: was the blood flowing through his body responding and reacting to being 'back home'? Or was it just a simple reaction to a place that had borne witness to the beginning of a trail of destruction that would last over 340 years? It did make me wonder if his heart somehow realised that his body had a direct connection to the land. Did one of my father's ancestors board a ship from that land never to set foot on it again, which would mean that, much like Claude McKay details in his poem, my dad 'had returned'?

That brings me back to the poem that we started this introduction with. Let me explain: I was sat in my hotel room in Kingston, Jamaica, when my producer handed me a photocopy of Claude McKay's poem. We'd been in the country a couple of days and were finally out of quarantine and able to start filming. The producer and I had become quite close by this point: we had been filming together for a few months and the quirks of genealogy programmes meant that she knew way more about my family history than I did at this point. She knew what I was about to find out over the next few days but couldn't tell me. Regardless, she had to prepare me emotionally.

We were sat in the hotel room by the windows looking out over the ever-vibrant colours of Kingston, with Blue Mountain peeking out in the distance. Everything just seems so bright in Jamaica; it's almost like someone tweaked the landscape with an Instagram filter in order to perfect its brilliance, which brings such a level of beautiful calmness.

She asked me to read the poem and explained that there was a connection to my story but couldn't give me any more detail. She just wanted me to take a look and familiarise myself with it. I remember nonchalantly glancing over it, more concerned with getting on with the filming that we were planning to do that day. Knowing me well enough by that point in proceedings, she told me to sit down, read it through a few more times and try to internalise the words, and the rhythm of the piece. I, once again, glanced over it, then folded it up and popped it in my backpack. Not doing exactly as I'm told, or just doing things my own way, is possibly not one of my better personality traits.

Fast-forward to the final filming day in Jamaica. By this point I had found out a lot about my family history including finding out who was the slave owner responsible for the family surname, 'Stanbury', as well as learning more about the family that came from him. We'd been able to go back to the 1700s – further than most descendants of enslaved people are fortunate enough to be able to do. I was standing at the top of a hill in Clarendon, a spa town in the south of Jamaica, talking to a genealogist who would reveal the final piece of my family puzzle. We were doing it slap-bang in the middle of the midday sun (and yes, I sang 'Mad Dogs and Englishmen' several times that day), so I was hot and bothered. I'd taken in a lot of information in the lead-up to that day, so I was mentally exhausted too. I'd learnt so much about the needs and wants of my family: what they'd been through and the path they'd taken in order to survive and take charge of their own lives. So, I was probably a lot more emotional that I'd realised. If you've ever had the opportunity to properly trace back your ancestry, you may agree that it's more of an emotional roller coaster than you ever thought it would be. And those emotions were bubbling away under the surface without me even realising. Even if I *was* aware, I was too tired and too hot to deal with it so I was in a constant battle trying to push the emotions back down until I had the headspace to properly deal with them.

Much like my dad's reaction in Kunte Kinteh Island, my body started taking over in ways I've never experienced before. As the genealogist started explaining my connection to Clarendon and this piece of land, internally my head and my heart were in the midst of an epic battle. My emotions trying to bubble to the surface, my brain fighting them back down. I really wasn't comfortable showing my emotions on screen. It's an alien concept for me. I steadfastly didn't want to do it.

The genealogist told me that day that we were standing by the small piece of land my ancestors bought in Clarendon when they became free, at an age not dissimilar to mine – their early forties. They made a choice to no longer financially depend on slave owners; they wanted to take charge of their own lives and start again at a place called Nairne Castle. It was a former plantation owned by Daniel Nairn, who had 150 enslaved people working on the property. After emancipation it became a Free Village, with the farm divided up among twenty previously enslaved families. This allowed them to work on their *own* small pieces of land and begin to create lives, and a future, in which they were in charge of themselves, as opposed to being property belonging to their owners.

This became the biggest marker of freedom for those who had spent their entire lives being someone else's property. They'd spent a lifetime being forced to work for the benefit of others, on land which had become synonymous with trauma, death, violence, coercion and exploitation. But it was also the land that would signal the beginning of something new, a tangible way to wipe the slate clean, and set in stone the development and growth of not just themselves, but of future generations – from the ashes of a trade that had destroyed so many previous generations. This is where the creation of Free Villages became instrumental, but there were stumbling blocks along the way. As you can imagine, getting hold of land was hard due to plantation owners *feeling* bruised by the changes in the law and reeling from their human cash cows walking away. So they were of little to no help, unsurprisingly (but let's not feel too sorry for them, eh? Britain was still paying its debt to slave owners until 2015. And the compensation package helped to secure the legacies of some of the most monied families in Britain today.) It fell on Christian missionary groups, and the few plantation owners whose consciences couldn't cope with the guilt, to help the now-formerly enslaved to cement their rebirth through land.[2]

The missionaries would buy up large swathes of land, and then divide them up for sale. The whole idea was created following the 'Ejectment' and 'Trespass Acts', which meant that enslaved families could be thrown off the ex-owner's land with just a week's notice, leaving them homeless and without work – but let's not forget that these were homes in which they had been born and lived in their entire lives. The creation of Free Villages no doubt saved countless lives across the Caribbean.

In the case of Nairne's Castle, Daniel left his plantation to his partner Sara William who was Black (they couldn't marry because it was illegal). They had six sons together, and Daniel left the land to Sara upon his death in 1816. It wasn't until the abolition of slavery in 1833 that she could officially become the owner. Andrew and Elsey and their children were among the twenty families who lived on the divided-up farm. So too was the family of Claude McKay, who was born in 1889. The emotional and physical impact of moving your life from enslaved to free is demonstrated by the long and fruitful lives both Andrew and Elsey lived atop that hill in Clarendon. They lived out their years at Nairne's Castle, with their family. Elsey died in 1878, age 'unknown but very old'. Andrew died in 1885, aged ninety.

Their decision to buy a plot of land and become a part of the Free Village movement, rather than continue to work on the land of the person who had owned them since birth, meant that they *knew* they were worth more, that they wanted to be more, and that they *deserved* more from their lives. These are traits that have permeated throughout my family, generation after generation.

That afternoon, I was stood under the beating sun, looking over the land which had not only enabled my great-great-great-great-grandparents Andrew and Elsey Pusey to start again, but marked the start of a new life for all the generations that followed: it was as beautiful as it was magical.

The view from the top of Clarendon is just stunningly perfect. It's as green as green can be, as far as the eye can see, with the peaks and troughs of the mountains opposite blurring into one. You can hear the faint sound of streams running through the mountains, you can smell the faint smell of the sweetsop and mangoes, you can see the spindly stalks of the yams growing, the callaloo spouting out the ground. You can hear the birds shouting at each other in the stillness, the dogs barking at everything and nothing. The sound system that had been cranked up loudly from the moment we arrived started blasting out Chevelle Franklyn & Lady G's 'Thank You', with the heavy bass reverberating against what felt like the sides of every hill we could see, and in all honesty at that point I think it was also probably reverberating against my heart. I was breathing but struggling to breathe, and my heart was pounding. It was the perfect storm for what happened next. I was struggling to take it all in, and I was desperately trying to calm myself down, when the genealogist finally explained the connection to Claude McKay.

The genealogist told me that McKay was a Jamaican poet

who was instrumental in the Harlem Renaissance but was born in Clarendon. On the drive up to Clarendon we had passed the high school that bears his name. His family also started again, once freed from enslavement, in Nairn's Castle, so his family and my family would've been neighbours: two families starting their lives with no idea of the ripple effect their decisions would have in terms of the quality of the lives of future generations.

I was then handed 'I Shall Return' and asked to read it aloud, the opening lines of course starting:

I shall return again; I shall return
To laugh and love and watch with wonder-eyes
At golden noon the forest fires burn,
Wafting their blue-black smoke to sapphire skies.

I could barely continue beyond that first line, the significance of his words suddenly hitting home. *I* had returned. I had returned to this piece of land which had seen so much violence and death, but which then became a place of hope. I had returned. And then came that final line, which broke me.

I shall return, I shall return again,
To ease my mind of long, long years of pain.

And that's when I just crumbled. I felt like the pain of my ancestors was flowing through my veins. I had returned to this spot with *their* blood, *their* DNA, but, like them, a free woman – the only difference is I was the ancestor who'd returned having only known a life of freedom. And it genuinely felt like I had returned to let those ancestors know that the long years of pain that they had endured had not been repeated. That their family was content and at peace.

Everything I'd been feeling from the moment I got out of the car in Clarendon, everything I'd been feeling throughout my time in Jamaica, it all suddenly came to a deafening crescendo when I read Claude's words. Without wanting to, without meaning to, without even realising I was doing it . . . I just started crying. A proper, guttural cry from the pit of my stomach, as though I was crying out pain that I didn't know I had inside me. Like I was letting go of the generational pain that had been sitting dormant for centuries. Everything that I'd been trying to push down exploded to the surface and I collapsed into my producer's arms. I had returned home.

Chapter 1

The Battle of Two Islands

Being the child of immigrants can be an often-constant tug of war in your heart and your head. You tentatively walk a tightrope between being enough of a representation of the country and culture of your parents' birth, while also trying to successfully assimilate into the country and culture of your *own* birth. Despite it being a battle that can leave your heart battered, bruised and scarred … there are no winners. How can there be? It's akin to a kids' superhero cartoon like *Teenage Mutant Ninja Turtles*, where the characters are faced with a challenge which they overcome at the end of each episode – but then when the next episode begins, something else is thrown in their direction and they have to navigate their way through in order to succeed, again. When your home is two distinct characters which you're trying to successfully balance, the cultural conundrums can feel never-ending. As you conquer one, another is thrown in your direction.

The tapestry of identity is complicated. Imagine the long tapestry of your own life hanging up in a museum. As you stand in front of it, taking in the wealth of images and pictures that represent you, which pictures and moments collectively tell the whole story of you? As you step forward to take a closer look, walking the length of the tapestry, the light catching images that make you smile or hit your heart, as your fingers brush against the intricate detailing of the weaving, what in those pictures shows your identity? For me, it's not just about the interesting moments in my life, it's also about representing the mix of me: the cultures and traditions that melted together to make me who I am. But as I walk the length of the tapestry of my own life, which pictures should take precedence in terms of the cultures that created me – the Jamaican side or the English side? For me, which seems more like home?

See, there we are. Back in battle once again.

Having parents who come from somewhere else is a real blessing. Life is just never bland or vanilla. From the moment I popped out of my mum that one Sunday morning in June 1980 in Greenwich, I was never going to just blend in. I was the child of two black immigrants. I was different. I was a minority. Our food was different, our weekend routines were different, how we spoke to grown-ups was different, our churches were different, our house parties were different, our weddings, funerals and christenings were different. I could go on. Culturally we were polar opposites of the English (but very similar to the Irish). And I loved it. It seemed like we lived a more exciting life than some of the white kids I went to school with. Our lives were colourful and vibrant and loud. All attributes that seemed to irk the English. But Jamaican immigrants didn't care. They were vehemently determined to hang onto their culture. It's a culture they'd *had* to create out of nothing.

Let's not forget that the majority of Jamaicans come from

Sub-Saharan Africa (it's thought to be almost 80 per cent), and most notably from what is now known as Ghana. They were dragged across to the other side of the world by boat, dumped in fields and forced to work for free. They were enslaved. Dehumanised, brutalised, stripped of all dignity. But when everything you know and love is taken away from you, you have to find joy somewhere, anywhere. Life without any joy equals no real existence. And that's where the creation of culture and tradition comes into play. When your home is taken away, you find joy by placing your stamp on the world with traditions and cultures that the generations that follow will continue to hold onto to feel grounded. To feel whole. To feel like they belong to something bigger than themselves.

My grandparents being *invited* to Britain to help after the war, rather than being *forced* to come here didn't mean that the need to hold onto that culture was lessened in any shape or form. Despite probably being more British than the English when they got here (my grandparents were British subjects, who were educated in a British education system in Jamaica), they were made to feel like anything but. They were unwelcome outsiders in so many different ways. This, despite the fact they had been *asked* to help the motherland rebuild itself having been ravaged by war. When you've moved to a new country to help, and the reaction is less than welcoming, it must have seemed strange back then. Although time hasn't lessened the bizarreness of that situation, to be honest.

The death toll after the Second World War was high. With 384,000 soldiers killed in combat and 70,000 civilian deaths (largely due to German bombing raids during the Blitz), this left a huge gap in terms of the people needed to help the country get back on its feet. Not only that, but the total working population had also dropped by 1.38 million between mid-1945 and the end of 1946. This was caused by many things, including families emigrating post-war, and the high numbers of married women and retirement-age workers who'd taken on roles during the war but now wanted to return to 'normal' life.[1]

And that's where the (almost former) British Empire came in handy. Having colonies all over the world hugely benefitted the British; it provided the country with valuable materials like metals, sugar and tobacco, a raft of money-making opportunities for wealthy Brits, and manpower for both the First and the Second World Wars. Advantages which were rarely, if ever, passed onto the indigenous communities.

The Second World War changed much of that, though, and not only altered Britain's view of its 'Empire', but also how the world viewed it. The war had left the country weakened and economically broken – not the biggest selling points for an empire – and so, the remaining parts of what was the British Empire eventually became the Commonwealth. This, despite Winton's Churchill's 1942 protestations: 'We mean to hold our own. I have not become the King's first minister in order to preside over the liquidation of the British Empire.'

In an ideal scenario, I would have imagined that former majority-white colonies like Australia and New Zealand would have been the British government's preferred choice for workers (less of a 'visual' shock to the locals, if you see what I mean), but both countries were also on the hunt for workers and had tapped into their old colonial black book and lured white British families over with treats like hot weather and beaches. And so, rather than getting neighbours who would 'throw another shrimp on the barbie', the British government got an oil drum, jerk chicken and Scotch bonnets. The 'clutching of pearls' action must have been epic.

With the white former colonial nations effectively 'out of office' by 1948 – three years after the Second World War ended – Britain needed to reach out to the Caribbean for help. This coincided with the 1948 Nationality Act which gave people from the Commonwealth the right to live and work in Britain if they wanted to.[2]

And that's where my grandparents, their children and thousands of others enter the equation when they made the journey. My grandparents and my Aunty Eleanor first arrived in the early 60s – my uncles and my mum arrived later. They are part of what is known as the 'Windrush generation', those who arrived in Britain from the Commonwealth between 1948–1971. Britain went on a recruitment drive in Jamaica to plug the gaps created by war: in the steel and coal industry, iron, food, construction, the health service, public transport. The list was endless, but it proved to be a lucrative offer to those who had high aspirations thousands of miles away on that little island in the Caribbean. However, it was mutually beneficial: Jamaicans were able to start new lives and better their economic situations, while Britain – with help from the Caribbean – was able to rise from the ashes of war.

So . . . you'd think there would be a level of understanding, a level of compassion, a level of . . . I dunno . . . gratitude, maybe? But as is prevalent the world over, the immigrant story is rarely told from a position of gratitude on behalf of the host nation. If it were, then 'Immigrant Saviour Complex' would be a thing. And yet, it's not.

For millions of Jamaicans/British subjects, Britain was 'home' and Elizabeth II was their Queen too, so coming here felt akin to 'coming home' – for that was the basis of colonial propaganda of the time. In their minds they were joining an extension of family, an imperial family of sorts which would welcome them with open arms. They were after all British citizens, but in official papers they were called 'coloured colonial labour', therefore immediately ostracising them as being inferior to other British workers. The language of colonialism set in stone an attitude towards them which is still felt by many of their descendants even today. Much like the immigrants that followed, they ended up in jobs far lower down the scale than their skills should have placed them.

This meant that those who came were restricted in the employment they could take up once they arrived: mostly in manufacturing and construction, transport and the NHS (as nurses and nursing aides. Not doctors, obviously.). Now imagine if the situation had been completely reversed: the immigrants invited to help rebuild this great nation had been welcomed with the open arms of a country that was in dire straits, inserted into jobs for which they were qualified, and offered the same opportunities as the white British. Just imagine the leg-up this would have given a country that was trying so desperately to retain its position as a small but mighty nation, capable of taking over the world.

My grandad was excited about accepting the invitation to come here and help rebuild the motherland, excitement that was tempered the moment he arrived. Racist Brits are very good at cutting you down to size. My educated and intelligent grandad was treated as anything but – and the jobs that should have been made available to him were at arm's length for ever. To racist Brits, his beautiful dark brown skin meant that he was obviously dumb and uneducated. It didn't matter how much he tried to convince them otherwise – racists are very good at behaving like children: sticking their fingers in their ears and refusing to listen. So he had to rebuild his life from the very bottom.

Although my grandad wasn't enslaved when he moved here, there were no doubt parts of him that were stolen by a system that *needed* him but didn't *want* him. It's like abuse on a massive scale: the system and its people constantly trying to chip away at any semblance of self-worth, self-belief and pride to maintain control, by using laws, policies and impassioned speeches to ensure the immigrants didn't get ideas above their station. All to ensure that immigrants didn't entrench themselves too much into British life, because to do that would signal the end of white Britain and its culture as we knew it. Utter drivel and rubbish, obviously. It will never cease to amaze me that that's literally the definition of colonisation. And as we know, in the Colonisation Olympics of old, Britain was the gold medal winner repeatedly for generations. The irony never fails to make me smile. Although it's amazing how whiffs of the propaganda of the past still reek in the modern day.

In the midst of all of this rejection in British society, my grandad and his friends holding on for dear life to the parts of their lives and culture that felt familiar became ever-more urgent. They were thousands of miles away from home, living in a country that consistently and brutally kept taking their hearts, twisting them until they hurt, and shattering them into a million pieces. That kind of pressure must have been unbearable at times, especially when you're trying to raise a family, and desperate to make the move across the Atlantic work out.

But rather than let it break them – and it broke many immigrants that came before and after them – they successfully sought solace in a culture that brought them joy: the reminders of home. Britain had taken so much from them; they were determined to not give them the pleasure of taking absolutely everything. Because to do that would mean they'd won. And in the immigrant battle, the oppressor can't win. They just can't. Because what then is left?

And so the battle to keep 'home' – to keep Jamaica – alive within their own four walls, churches, and social circles became imperative to their own mental health. Although the concept of preserving one's mental health wasn't on anyone's radar in the '60s and '70s, that's exactly what my grandparents and their friends were doing: bringing a slice of Jamaica to south-east London to preserve their mental health. Without it, the clouds of depression and madness that were always swirling around in the air above them would eventually engulf them, as it did so many immigrants of the time, the pressure proving too much. Those dark clouds were always in touching distance, and were you to give in, you ran the risk of your mind being lost for ever.

My grandad was a man of faith, so an obvious place of solace would've been Britain's many churches. I can imagine him arriving here in cold dark Britain with all its prejudice and racism, and thinking, 'At least I have my faith. This too shall pass.' I can imagine him in his crisp suit, trilby hat, shiny shoes, clutching his ever-present Bible, and heading for the first church he could find, only to realise that the OG racists resided within the walls of churches.

Racism masked as faith permeated through Britain's religious systems like a cancer: immigrants of faith and of all denominations were rejected en masse. But so strong was my grandad's faith and that of his friends, they did what countless other immigrants did across the country – they created their own churches. First in their homes, then in whatever halls they could find. They needed to. For those with strong faith and beliefs, God grounded them. The words of the Bible kept them sane and brought them joy like no other. Faith is one of the things they held onto for dear life on that journey from Jamaica to England. They had their suitcases, their pictures, their trinkets, but in their hearts was their faith, which was probably the most important thing. No one could take it from them, and it gave them hope. Hope that uprooting their families and moving them to the other side of the world wouldn't be the worst decision of their lives.

Oh, the beauty of Black immigrant churches (also now known as Black Majority Churches). If you've never been to one, my gosh, you've missed out – it's euphoric. Even if you're not a believer, you will be guaranteed to feel some kind of spiritual awakening. A good preacher will lift your soul and have you shouting loudly in agreement as they masterfully spread the word. A great gospel choir will hit your heart so hard you have no control over the emotional reaction to it. This is the environment I grew up in every weekend ... for hours and hours every Sunday. The church van would do the rounds of south-east London picking up the kids from various locations, then drop them off at church for Sunday school, the parents making their own way there later on, for the main service.

That's why the majority of a traditional Caribbean Sunday dinner had to be cooked *before* church on a Sunday, as you had no idea what time you'd be back. A short service could go on and on for hours, and as a kid it just seemed never-ending and tortuous. But looking back, growing up in the church helped to shape who I am. It added to the Caribbean cultural education that my parents so desperately wanted us to have. In their younger years, my parents had grown up in a society in which visually they were equals. But then they'd been moved by their parents to a country where they became an unwanted and unequal minority, whose culture was endlessly mocked, whose traditions were belittled, and whose very existence offended so many. It was important for them and others to hold onto their culture with a need that those who aren't immigrants may find hard to comprehend. It was about actual survival in a country which aimed to weaken you in any way it could find.

And church was instrumental in that survival. For those of faith, having a space in which they could worship in a way they felt safe and secure was so important. If you're a person of faith, you know it's the thing that you hold onto in both your happiest and lowest moments. Some days you have to hold onto it for dear life, because it can fill your heart with hope when you feel all is lost. It gives you hope that things *will* and *can* get better. It gives you hope that the ills of the world can be solved simply by having faith, that your heart can be filled with faith, that your family will be safe with faith. Faith in your darkest moment can be the light that you desperately seek. It's not for everyone, but when you see faith in action things can seem brighter, more whole.

Moving to the UK and the myriad difficulties that brought about for Caribbean immigrants would have tested that faith in so many different ways. There would have been a lot of darkness, and so they would have needed that faith more than ever. But then they would have walked into an English church which immediately turned them away. Let's not forget that's fundamentally against the teachings of any church. Matthew 25:35: 'For I was hungry and you gave me food, I was thirsty and you gave me drink, I was a stranger and you welcomed me.' Unless you were Black, of course.

My nanny and grandad's generation would have been heartbroken. But their heartbreak and that of many other Caribbean immigrants started a wave of immigrants carving out their own religious spaces that continues today. As English churches continue to fight any hint of change and modernisation (you'd think after decades they'd have eased up a bit), BMCs (Black Majority Churches) are thriving, and quite ironically they've been the savour of religion in the UK. As mainstream churches continue their steady decline, and therefore the fundamentals of the faith that makes England a Christian country, BMCs are experiencing the opposite. Ironic doesn't seem like a strong enough description, to be honest. Through their own internalised racism, mainstream churches missed their opportunity to create a beautiful tapestry of faith which would allow *all* through its doors. Its rejection of that has played a hand in the lessening of its relevance, and it could have all been avoided.

Pre-war, the first BMC in Europe was founded in London: the Sumner Road Chapel in Peckham, south London, in 1906. It was created by Rev Thomas Kwame Brem-Wilson who emigrated from Ghana to Britain in 1901. His was among the first Pentecostal churches in Britain. Post-war, the first of the Caribbean Pentecostal churches was founded in 1948, the Calvary Church of God in Christ, also in London.[3] The city is now one the most religious in the country, with Black churchgoers accounting for 48 per cent of attendees.[4] Again, ironic just doesn't seem strong enough.

Some may argue that it was my grandparents and those of that generation's failure to assimilate that's caused the issue. But the English churches of the time actively turned them away, refused to see the benefits of assimilating two cultures through the prism of religion, and rejected any notion of using faith as a vehicle to deal with racism head-on. If they had followed the teachings of the Bible and not used religion to legitimise their own racism and bigotry, it makes you wonder how different England would be now. Churches were, and still are, the gatekeepers. There's a lot of hate that could have been averted if the religious powers that be had made different, more accepting, choices.

But in the face of all this, my grandparents and their friends didn't choose to exist purely on anger. They didn't lose their faith. I'm not sure I would have had the same level of strength and composure. Instead, they kept their faith and launched their own churches, because they had to. Holding onto their faith kept them sane; it was their version of preserving their mental health. And I'm thankful for them doing that, because my education in the church for all those years wasn't just about learning the teachings of the Bible – it was also everything that we learnt about ourselves and about each other outside of Sunday school. In Black churches the older members of the congregation are referred to as brothers and sisters. They were children of God and referred to each other as such.

For example, one of my nanny's closest friends was always addressed as 'Sister Ward'. Whether I was talking to Sister Ward inside the walls of the church or while wandering around Lewisham Market with my friends, she was always 'Sister Ward'. In fact, I don't think I could have actually told you what Sister Ward's first name was at the time. That's because it didn't matter then or now. Why would it? And that's the respect that we all held as kids and still do for those within the church community. It's ingrained and will never change.

It was the church brothers and sisters who'd immediately call your parents if they saw you misbehaving on the street. So not only did you have to worry about your parents catching you hanging around Lewisham Shopping Centre after school, you had any number of the hundreds of church folk scattered about south-east London. Mobile phones had yet to become a thing on the streets back then, but that didn't matter much. The Black church grapevine was probably way more efficient and definitely faster than any modern technology. The ability of church brethren to fill your parents in on any bad behaviour they witness in record time was honestly a thing of beauty. Well, I can say that now, because I'm not on the receiving end. But back then you'd have to constantly look over your shoulder even if you dared to *talk* to a boy that wasn't in the church. Life would become very difficult if you were spotted. To tell the truth, times were hard back then.

But behind the admonishments for talking too loudly during the sermon, or coughing too loudly, or sneezing too loudly, or moving in your seat too loudly, there was so much love. Love that you just can't replicate. These are men and women who aren't related to you by blood but who will be family for ever. It was the church sisters who sat and prayed with my mum and aunt when my nanny became sick with cancer; it was church family both old and new who surrounded my mum when she too was struck with the same illness. From first thing in the morning till last thing at night, they sat by her bed, held her hand and prayed with her. Even though she wasn't lucid, I know how much that would have meant to her. It taught me about the community outside of the walls of my family. It taught me that we are more than the sum of our surnames and blood, that community can be as loving as family, and can be just as responsible for holding us together in moments when we feel broken.

And this is what my grandparents and so many of that generation were so desperate to hold onto when they moved to England. Because the joy and love of community meant even more to them here. So many of their family members were still back in Jamaica – some had decided not to take up the offer of work in the UK, while others were waiting their turn. But in the absence of family, any way to create an environment in which they felt safe and secure was held onto with both hands. For my grandparents, that was church. Irrespective of what was thrown at them outside of church, inside those walls was a love that was unmatched. A community that would always hold them up, who would never turn them away, who would use their faith as a vehicle of acceptance. It was a lifeline which helped preserve their sanity, and no doubt saved their lives.

As a result of having been raised solely in Caribbean churches, I hadn't experienced a 'regular' English church until the latter years of primary school when we had to go to one for a carol service. Before then I'd only walked past them in the street. And they seemed strangely eerie. They were just quiet from the outside! It was quite unnerving. You could hear organs every now and then, but you could barely hear the congregation. The sounds from the outside never quite tempted me in to see what it was like. So, my first carol service with the school at All Saints, on Blackheath, was quite the revelation.

My gosh. We sang, yes. But it was different. It was lacking, for want of a better word, any soul. There were no drums, no trumpets, no guitars. There was zero band! And the pacing of songs was just so . . . slow. *Excruciatingly* slow. It was really quite bizarre. And no one clapped to the beat while they were singing. I mean, the pace was so slow it was nigh-on impossible anyway. But still! It just all seemed so . . . 'meh'. I couldn't understand how people did *this* on a weekly basis.

And there wasn't a single 'Hallelujah!' shouted from the congregation. Not a single one! Church isn't church without several indiscriminate hallelujahs yelled from church sisters in too-large hats with their eyes closed and their arms raised while they sway from side to side as they're consumed by the spirit of the Lord. Black church isn't just one thing, it's the sum of a million different things happening all at once. It's never quiet. Faith isn't quiet where I'm from. Faith is loud, it's joyous, it's colourful. It's the polar opposite of the grey walls and quiet of English churches. And that's why, although sitting in churches remains one of my favourite things, the quiet of traditional English churches still unnerves me. It feels strange. Without all that background noise swirling around in the walls of a church, it just doesn't work for me.

I, however, don't go to church as often as I should. And I know my mum and grandparents no doubt turn in their graves on a regular basis as a result. Though growing up within the walls of various churches across south-east London means that my heart will be entwined with it for ever, my heart doesn't always sit well with the church's teachings. For many people who were regular churchgoers in the '80s and '90s, it was a time when intolerance of anyone who was 'different' was positively encouraged rather than understood, most specifically the demonising of those in the LGBTQ+ community ... alongside the reluctance to have women in senior positions in the church. Although one could argue that, on the whole, that battle continues.

Does the church, then, feel like home to me? Well, yes. I guess it does. And that's because of my faith. I may rarely step into churches these days but that's the great thing about faith – it's not based on a physical structure. It's a beautiful thing that can make my heart sing. There are certain Bible scriptures that can catapult me straight back to being a kid, squashed into one of the pews with my mum and her church sisters, vaguely listening to the pastor give his sermon high up on the pulpit, daydreaming about what else I *could* be doing that Sunday instead. But what I didn't realise then, but I know for sure now, is that through some weird osmosis, his words were getting into my heart and my head. And I remember them even today.

I am under no illusion that not everyone reading this will come from a position of having faith and spending most of their childhood being raised in the church, and so may not understand the depth of this faith. It was such an integral part of my grandparents' life here, and then for their children, that faith and home are hugely intertwined for me. And it's difficult to pull them apart. It's like planting two different seeds into a pot, and them becoming a hybrid plant. I suppose in a weird way I'm that hybrid, like so many others in a similar situation.

Like I've mentioned before, it was faith and scripture that kept my grandparents going. It's no exaggeration to say that those thousands of words written across the thin pages of those leather-bound books kept my grandparents' hearts beating with hope that things would get better here. Like 1 Corinthians 13:4-6: 'Love is patient, love is kind.' Or Matthew 17:20: 'Our faith can move mountains.' Or Psalm 23:4: 'Even though I walk through the valley of the shadow of death, I fear no evil, for You are with me; Your rod and Your staff, they comfort me.'

The words of the Bible would guide my grandparents through the maze that was life as a first-generation immigrant in the UK. It would be his faith that would get my grandad's tired body out of bed every morning to go to work, a faith that was reinforced by him briefly touching the cross nailed to the wall by the front door as he left the house. The same cross he'd briefly touch again when he walked back into the house after a long day. He was thankful to the Lord every single day for keeping him and his family safe. 'Praise the Lord,' and 'Thank you, God,' were phrases we heard him say under his breath routinely.

Although my grandparents moved here in the 1960s, seeking solace in faith as a newly arrived immigrant is a thread that continues today. For all the church's protestations of being accepting of difference (Leviticus 19:34 for example: 'The foreigners residing among you must be treated as native-born. Love them as yourself, for you were foreigners in Egypt. I am the Lord your God.'), there is still so much division that can make recent immigrants feel unwanted and unwelcome. However, much like my grandparents, from the moment they walk into a religious building, an immigrant of faith can instantly find both a home and hope – whoever they pray to. That's what my grandparents and their friends created with their churches: a home away from home, as they created new lives . . . away from the home of their birth.

But home for them stretched beyond the walls of the church, obviously. Yes, church was where they could seek solace and strength among their friends. But creating a home in England, albeit temporarily for many Jamaican immigrants, was about more than that. From food, to music, to culture, building a home here needed all those elements too. If you're a child of immigrants, having a combination of all those things aides that feeling of having a dual home.

It's why, even now, I can step off the plane in Jamaica and immediately feel at home. My soul feels alive the moment I walk out the door of the airport. I breathe in that warm sweet air, and suddenly I'm enveloped by its culture and its people. *My culture. My people.* Do I get that feeling when I land in London? Not really, and that's not because it means less. It's because landing in Jamaica is like collapsing with joy into the arms of a relative: one you love with all your heart but don't get to see often. England, though it's in my heart, is a bit like a relative you see every day ... you love them to bits, and probably take them for granted. But there's a huge difference between stepping into a country where you're the majority, to living in a country where you are the minority: a huge, cavernous difference. When you live every day looking different from the majority and standing out *on a daily basis* – because of something you have no control over – and are treated as such, you *do* live differently. When you step off a plane and are visually in the majority, you walk a little straighter, your shoulders a little higher.

A lot of that feeling is linked to the way I was raised in London. I'm a child of immigrants who never lost their connection to the home of their birth. It was important for them to maintain that connection, and for their children to understand that who they were was based on more than simply being born in England. They were the sum of two worlds and two cultures: it was complicated, but beautiful.

I grew up in England, I was raised in a quintessentially Jamaican household. That involved everything from Caribbean discipline, food, music, culture, manners ... the list is endless, really. But my favourite on that list was food. No one would ever leave our house hungry. Even if you had nothing, you would use whatever little you had to hand to make something for guests, even unexpected ones. My parents taught me that in Jamaican culture, someone leaving your house hungry is a huge marker of disrespect. And we're not talking finger sandwiches, we're talking a full-on meal. We show love through food, because coming from the level of poverty that many Jamaicans grew up in, food was the only way to show love.

Back then, you couldn't just pop to your local supermarket and grab the ingredients you needed to create Jamaican dishes (and you still can't really), so on a Saturday morning, I'd be up early to do my chores (cleaning, hoovering, and polishing the living room and kitchen) and then we'd head out to the market. I think it's important for me to state here, going to market wasn't an afternoon exploit. It would be done first thing – at a push you'd be there around 10 a.m. Any later, and my mum would be fuming. So that would mean I'd have to be up at the crack of dawn, make the family fried plantain and eggs for breakfast, do my chores, and be dressed and ready by the latest at 9 a.m. to head to the market to do the weekly shopping. And my mum didn't take any tardiness. We'd get a cussing if we made her late for market.

Having perused the markets in Jamaica with various aunties (although, 'being dragged around' the markets is probably the more appropriate phrase to use), I can completely understand the attraction of Lewisham Market and Lewisham Black Market on a Saturday morning. It would've felt like home to them. The main market was your typical English Market (but so few of them exist in London now), an explosion of colour and noise: men and women belting out prices at the top of their lungs trying to entice you to their stall to buy their beautiful and vibrant fruit and veg. Older ladies pulling their shopping trolley behind them as they wander from stall to stall looking for the best deals. The annoyance of disgruntled stallholders as buyers started to barter. The smell of boxes and boxes of fresh produce lined up at the front of stalls like multicoloured chequerboards. The sounds of portable radios stashed at the back of stalls as their owners sit and wait for another rush of customers. The smell of cigarettes as stallholders somehow manage to serve, pack, hold long conversations and tell jokes, all while a fag hung precariously from their lips.

As you walked further towards the Black Market, you'd start passing the meat stalls and the fishmonger stalls, and the meat shops. As a kid it was the part of the shopping trip that I disliked the most because of the smell, and, you know ... the dead chickens and goats and various other animals hanging from hooks. But in order to get to the part of the trip I *loved* the most, I had to suck it up. I don't think my mum ever bought meat from the supermarket back then. It was always from the market, because the market had the cuts of meat she was after, unlike high street supermarkets who were not well known for their goat meat, goats head, oxtail, cow feet and chicken feet back then. And curiously still aren't. It was to the market you had to go so that you could rustle up something nice.

But only particular stalls, mind. Not all meat stalls are created equal on a market. If I accidentally bought from the wrong stall or shop, I'd get yet another cussing. Buy meat from the wrong stall or shop and you're destined for a runny belly for days. You really couldn't take your chances.

We were fortunate enough to have a long strip of market (it's depleted somewhat now), with a lot of choose from. But at the end of the strip, that was where the best part of the market always appeared. This was where we got the good stuff, and was by far my favourite part of the trip.

The Black Market's name was self-explanatory, but in two ways. Yes, it was because it was the place to pick up West Indian food and products, but it also got his name from

Brenda Black and her husband who ran businesses inside it. So the 'Black Market' just became its name, and I never heard it being called anything else. In fact, I didn't know it was *actually* called the 'Model Market' until some twenty years later when the market itself was long gone, as gentrification came tentatively knocking at the door of Lewisham and street-food stalls moved in.

The Black Market was the place you would go to buy the Black stuff that supermarkets routinely refused to stock (and some still do). This is where mum would buy yams, green bananas, sweet potatoes, mangoes, bammy, cassava, etc., etc.: her food from home, Jamaica. Those bright blue plastic shopping bags would be stuffed full of Jamaican food to take home and turn into endless dishes that would fill the house with the smells of the Caribbean. Mum would stand and barter with the stallholder; she'd then bump into a million people she knew so we had to keep stopping so that she could chat. They would then ask me how school was going, and I, despite walking for what felt like hours, had to smile politely and answer without any hint of the fatigue that would frequently wave over me by this point. Any sign of annoyance or tiredness would warrant a massive telling-off when I got home, so I knew better than to complain. But also, the bit of the trip I loved the most was almost in touching distance – and not only that, I could smell it.

I can't tell you how much my hands hurt from the weight of carrying those bags, leaving the inside of my fingers with red indentations from the many handles digging into my skin. But you couldn't complain. Complaining would take the *best part of the trip* away before I'd even had a chance to glance nonchalantly in its direction. The only way to handle it was to smile through the pain, pretend that it didn't feel like your hand was about to be chopped in half. And pray really, really hard that you didn't drop one of the bags.

Once Mum had bought what we call 'hard food', we continued through the market. Slightly further up on the right-hand side was by far the best stall in there for a kid in their teens, it was where all the knock-off designer clothes were sold. The labels of the time back then were Karl Kani and FUBU. I'd walk past the stall admiring the knock-off wares in full knowledge that my parents wouldn't let me wear them (even knock-offs were too expensive back then), and hope that one day they wouldn't be in charge of my wardrobe and my money box.

But just as you were getting to the end of the knock-off stall, *the best part of the shopping trip* was straight ahead in all its glory. The patty stall. Right in front of the Black hair shop (I'll get to that in just a second) was where you could buy a beef patty. Displayed in a clear-sided warmer on top of shelving at the front of the stall were rows and rows of warmed patties, in all their yellow glory.

The smell. Oh my goodness, the smell. It's the smell of beef mince, cooked with myriad spices including cumin, curry powder, thyme and slivers of Scotch bonnet peppers, wrapped in the flakiest, most beautiful yellow pastry. The semi-circled pockets of goodness are then served very simply in a brown paper bag which is wrapped around the bottom half, soaking up the grease from the pastry, leaving a yellow head popping out the top ready for you to bite into.

And it's that first bite that you most look forward to. The

flakes stick around your mouth when you sink your teeth in. That first glorious bite then releases the heat inside, the steam hitting your lips at the same time the hot beef hits your tongue, burning both. It then leaves you waving your free hand in front of your mouth in a futile attempt to cool down the contents. No one waits for a patty to cool down before they eat it; that would be utter madness.

This was the moment that made being dragged around the markets worth it: being bought a fresh patty. Growing up, there were few things that could placate the child of Caribbean immigrants more than a patty on a Saturday. I'm not sure what the English alternative would be – maybe a burger from Wimpy or McDonalds or something. But we were allowed those things very infrequently. The grab-and-go snack of choice in a Jamaican house was a patty. And I adored them. Even now, the smell and taste of warm patties are still one of my favourite things. Maybe it's the nostalgia of what it represented back then. If I'd been naughty that week, or got bad results at school, I could only look at the patty stall wistfully from afar because I wouldn't be allowed one. But if I'd had a good week, the thought of getting my patty on a Saturday would genuinely fill me with great joy.

Now, of course, times have changed. Which may well have changed the excitement levels of grabbing a patty for kids now. You no longer have to wait for a Saturday visit to the market to grab one; you can, if the moment takes you, simply pop to Sainsburys to pick one up. However, for the uninitiated, it's important that I scream a point of clarification: a supermarket patty is a *very* poor relation to an actual patty. I promise you, I cannot emphasise that enough. If you're after the bliss that comes from biting into an insanely hot fresh patty, I beg you: please do not fill your basket with a Tesco knock-off. Your first must be authentically, burn-your-tongue fresh with that heady mix of spices and herbs encroaching up your nose. If you're used to delicate tastes, it's honestly just not for you. But if you like hot seasoning slapping you in the face, you will think of it as a thing of beauty: a feat that a supermarket version just fails to achieve. Plus, the meat to pastry ratio is so wrong, I'm not even sure how they passed any consumer testing. If I'm two bites into a patty and I haven't reached the meat yet, then it simply won't do. Anyway, I digress.

When I think back to it, grabbing a patty wasn't just a treat for me but for my parents too. They were able to bite into a slice of home while doing the Saturday shopping, a slice of something that my mum hadn't prepared herself. There were very few Caribbean takeaways around back then: when the government is actively dissuading banks from lending to Caribbean immigrants, getting any kind of business started was hard. Therefore, if my parents wanted the food from home, they had to do it themselves. But on a Saturday morning, within the beauty of the Black Market, someone else did it for her ... and to be honest, making patties at home takes for ever. Only once during my childhood did my aunt, my mum and I try to make them, and it took all evening – which honestly took the buzz out of the whole thing. You can't inflict patty-making on a patty-lover; the process is too long and the outcome is ... well ... let's put it this way: there's a reason why we bought them from the Black Market. There are some things that you just need to leave to the professionals.

Back to the market now, and as I mentioned the patty

stand stood right in front of the hair shop. So theoretically you could grab a patty, *and* buy the products for wash day the next day (in most households, the washing of Afro hair happens on a Sunday). I mean, it may not sound like the obvious merging of products in one location – food and hair – but Black hair products were sparse back then.

Despite being born and bred in London and considering it my home, the reminders of the clash and mismatch of British and Caribbean cultures was evident every single time I walked into a chemist, supermarket, or any other location that sold hair products (as well as any shop that sold make-up). It was another scenario where we were made to feel like we were a jigsaw piece that didn't quite fit correctly into the overall picture. Encouraged to assimilate, we were supposed to slip seamlessly into the puzzle that is the UK, but at every turn the edges of our pieces were not curved the right way, were too long or too short, too big or too small. And there's something to be said about a system that technically *discouraged* and simply ignored assimilation. Hair being evidence of that may seem like a wild concept, but only those *without* Afro hair would see it that way.

Unlike my friends at school who could waltz into any local high-street chemist to buy products to wash and condition their hair, finding *any* hair products in *any* regular high-street shop that was suitable for Afro hair was rarer than a blue moon. The shops simply weren't interested in stocking them. I'd walk down the aisles in Boots in Lewisham to grab cotton wool or soap and walk past rows and rows of products specifically aimed at hair that did not look or feel like mine, featuring pictures of men and women who didn't look like me.

These products weren't for me. Their claims of 'extra shine', or 'lengthening' or 'thickening' properties fell on deaf ears: without the ingredients, oils and moisture specifically aimed at my Afro, I'd be looking at a future with hair that was breaking and dry. Therefore, just about every single high-street shop was useless to me in terms of hair products. And it's strange how that was normalised, especially in hugely racially diverse cities like London, Bristol and Birmingham. Big name shops actively *chose* to ignore swathes of the population because they were deemed not worth the money and investment.

The joke now, of course, is that all these years later the penny has finally dropped as to the monetary value of the Black haircare market, with high-street shops up and down the country now falling over themselves to invest and stock as many ranges of hair products as possible. The numbers don't lie. The UK Black hair industry is worth an estimated £88 million, with Black women spending on average three times more than their white counterparts on hair care. And here's another interesting fact: Black women make up 80 per cent of the total hair product sales in the UK and spend six times more on cosmetics than any other ethnic group.[5]

And yet, it's only in recent years that I've been able to walk into a high-street shop and grab anything suitable for my hair. That light-bulb moment when CEOs realised precisely how much Black women spend must have been quite something. I was wandering around in Waitrose a few months ago and spotted that they too also now stock a Black haircare range, making me realise that the even the voices and wallets of the Black middle class were considered desirable now. Who'd have thought *that* would happen?

But what we see in our shops now is the exact opposite of what was on offer then. The small hair shops hidden away in corners of markets were a lifeline for so many of us. For those of us with Afro hair, one could argue that it was one of our emergency services, because without it I dread to think what state our hair would have been in. Although, give a Black woman a larder cupboard and she will knock up a homemade hair product capable of moisturising and softening those coily curls in no time. Just like so many other situations in life as a minority, you have to find a way around it. But why *should* we have to?

If you were lucky to have a family member visiting from the Caribbean, or the Black haircare Mecca of America, that's when you'd hit the jackpot. When my uncle or aunts would make the journey, added to the shopping list which included Black dolls would be haircare products, powerful hair dryers (which invariably wouldn't work because of the voltage difference), combs to heat up on the gas stove to straighten hair, and as many hair products as they could carry. Oh, the joy of dropping into conversation the name of the 'latest' American hair product that you were rocking in your hair, fresh off the plane from Miami.

But all that paled in comparison to actually *walking* into a shop that made you feel like you mattered. The Black hair shop was quite a sight to behold, seeing so many products specific to our race, which is a totally different experience to walking into a high-street shop. Although, when you walked over the threshold you'd be lucky if the owner acknowledged you. There wasn't much in the way of idle chit-chat, let alone a customary 'hello'. But that didn't matter, because what they did have was row upon row of products specifically made for me. For my hair. And if I'd been allowed (the owner didn't like browsing, he was more of a 'grab what you want and get out' kind of fella) I would have loved to have spent hours just walking round and looking at the labels. But it was too small for browsing and could only handle a handful of folk, if that. It was more shed-like in size rather than a high-street shop, so idle browsing meant losing money from the next customer. You had to be super quick in deciding what you needed, and then be ushered out. However, if you took a beat too long, the ushering-out vocabulary would be … let's say … slightly more demanding in nature.

But it was quite something to look up at those shelves and see nothing but pictures of models with hair that mimicked mine, with skin tones reflecting what I saw in the mirror every day. Crossing the threshold of the shop, I was suddenly transported into an environment that didn't constantly scream how different I was, and how much I stood out from the 'norm'. I could stand in the middle of this tiny stall and feel, well, normal. I could feel like a Black girl that sodding well deserved to also feel beautiful.

I'd stand behind my mum as she hurriedly chose what she wanted from the shelves, while I tried to not get patty flakes all over the floor, to not burn my tongue, and to still keep hold of the ridiculous number of blue plastic bags I'd been tasked with holding. And yes, it was as complicated as it reads. But it was a mission that I couldn't fail in, or I'd have had to deal with a telling-off in the middle of the market. Granted, you could always hear some kid being told off in the Black Market by their mum, especially on a Saturday morning. When you added together the various telling-offs, the stallholders calling out to customers trying to lure them in to buy products, and the soft bass of reggae playing from the entrance to the record shop, it all merged and moulded together into a soundtrack of blissful familiarity.

It's incredible how much can change in a generation. When I talk about pictures of hair that looked like mine, almost universally pictures were of women with poker-straight, long flowing hair: Black hair in its *unnatural* form. As in relaxed hair, as opposed to Black *natural* hair. As if there weren't enough hurdles to go over for Black immigrants, the hair conundrum is one that goes back to slavery.

Before the transatlantic trade begun, Black hair was braided and fashioned into styles that would reflect things like their age, marital status, wealth, religion, etc. What sat atop their heads carried weight: it was an important part of an individual. It could take days to create something so incredibly intricate and beautiful; it would be admired by all around. One of the first things the slave masters did to those they captured was to shave it all off, thus dehumanising further those who were being dragged away from the only life they knew, leaving any joy that existed in their world behind.

Their white slave master would refer to their hair as wool: with the oils, potions and combs left behind in West Africa, the condition of their hair once it grew back was rough and tangled. In the 1850s, the American architect and journalist Fredrick Law Olmsted wrote about his travels through South Carolina, and noted a scene in a campsite when he saw a father and son: 'An old negro [sat] with his head bowed down over a meal sack while the negro boy was combing his wool with a common horse-card.'[6] Black hair being referred to as 'wool' is peppered throughout the written history of the time. The lack of respect for Black hair in its natural state was something that continued, throughout generations, the Eurocentric standards of beauty determining not only your hierarchy on a plantation, but also the job prospects of Black women in the workplace centuries later. On the plantation, 'good hair' was characterised as that which was straighter, meaning enslaved people would go to extreme lengths to force their natural curls to fall downwards, rather than out. This process would involve butter knives being heated up on the fire, or chemical-based potions which would burn their skin. But it would be worth it for survival: 'good hair' would mean better jobs in the plantation house, your desirability having increased because your hair was more 'white'.[7]

But that is a situation that we still see today, which is the reason why growing up, the pictures plastered across Black haircare products of the time (and today) were mostly Black hair in its straighter, and what was/is perceived as its more desirable form. By the mid-'90s, when I was waltzing round the hair shop in the Black Market, the straightening tools of the trade were, again, chemical-based straightening creams and a hot comb. In order for immigrants such as my grandmas and my mum to fit into their new home, the conformity included one of the two above: the straightening creams which included ingredients such as alkali, ammonium thioglycolate or formaldehyde (first invented in 1909 by Garrett Augustus Morgan), or a metal comb which was heated up on a gas stove and then run through small sections of hair (invented by Francois Marcel Grateau in 1872, in France). The absence of either of those things to put through Black hair would mean knowingly putting yourself at even more of a disadvantage both at school and at work – and run the risk of being ridiculed by white colleagues or classmates routinely.

Michelle Obama is a good example of this phenomenon. During the eight years she was in office, the former First Lady wore her hair in a range of styles, but it was always straight. However, just a few months after leaving, she was spotted rocking her hair in its natural state for the first time: the shackles of conformity having been shed, finally. The reverberations could be felt by Black women the world over, and the understanding of *why* she'd waited so long didn't need to be uttered by anyone who understood.

If you stood in the middle of the main part of the Black Market and closed your eyes and just listened, I realise now that the sounds and smells that would hit you were akin to those of markets thousands of miles away, in lands where the weather was hotter. How lucky were we to have what felt like a corner of the Caribbean in a small labyrinth of stalls and shops in a market space in south London? If you stood in the middle facing the patty shop, you could hear the blow dryers in the Black hair salon to your left, accompanied by the loud voices of the women inside, laughing or cussing (or both). You could smell the chemicals of the straightening cream wafting from within as it hit the smell of the patties being cooked in front of you. And then you'd have the quiet solace of the Black greeting card shop behind you, and the vibrating bass of the record shop to your right. All of this, of course, would be interspersed with the constant, faint (and occasionally strong) smell of weed drifting through the market. A constant companion in this historic part of south-east London.

Rather than the often-frenetic nature of the English market just outside its walls, the hubbub in the Black Market was calmer, more soulful, less chipper, if that makes sense. It provided what the English market couldn't and wouldn't supply to us outside of its walls. Its sounds and smells have a steel grip on my heart because it represents a period in time for me before big business finally decided that certain aspects of Black culture sells, and sells well. It was a time when being routinely followed round shops by security guards was the norm for those of us with a darker hue, but in the Black Market you weren't assumed a thief the moment you walked in.

I often felt that the shops on the high street didn't want me or other Black people to frequent them. Luckily, we had shops that catered to Caribbean culture where I could feel comfortable. I'm trying to find the words to convey just what it's like to have industry upon industry pretend that you don't exist, to not bother catering to your needs, or provide you with suitable products – because the assumption is that you can't afford it. This presumption isn't just centred in the haircare industry but extends to the beauty industry too. The Body Shop's bronzing powder – my goodness, that stuff was a lifeline in my late teens. Why? Well, we Black girls were well used to having to make do with mismatched foundation and powders. Either you dug deep in your pockets for high-end Mac, or you had to make do with cheaper pressed powders that were created to make white skin look ... brown (and tanned). Yep, the irony isn't lost on me either.

Growing up in a country that seemed to enjoy reminding

you that it viewed you as different from what they viewed as the norm is a strange environment to exist in. In so many ways you were left at a disadvantage, especially economically. In modern language we call it being 'othered'. But the process of being othered can also have the unintended outcome of creating joy. The lack of embrace helped to create microcosms of Caribbean joy in cities up and down the country. And my gosh, with that came such beauty: strength is in numbers, as they say. That's why both inside my home and outside of it, I was raised Caribbean – the English bits existed in the periphery around that.

As beautiful as that was, as a young person I felt as though I was constantly trying to fight against so much of it. Especially when it came to discipline. Others seemed to have so much more freedom compared to me – and that was so hard. I was by no means the only Black kid that had to somehow manage that. Those of my friends who were of Caribbean and West African heritage all had the same struggles. Compared to many of our white English friends, we often felt as though we were trapped in a cage that we were rarely allowed to venture out of.

Back then, there was so much that angered me about how tough my parents were with me. Especially when I reached my early teenage years. There was a lot that my English friends were allowed to do that I just wasn't. I simply had to sit and listen as they regaled me with stories of their weekend exploits, while I felt like I was constantly locked in a cycle of school–sport–church–home. The grip loosened as I reached my late teens, but in the intervening years I wanted them to ease off on the Jamaican discipline and to chill out a bit, like my white English friends' parents. Although, as many first-generation born here will understand, 'chilled out' and 'parenting' are not terms that go hand in hand.

From what they could see looking out, and what my mum experienced as a social worker, and what my aunt experienced as a teacher, chilling out like white English parents was the exact thing that they were trying to prevent. That's what they were pushing back against. They didn't want me to become 'too' English and lose, as they saw it, the values that I had been raised with.

But it wasn't just that – they were also trying to keep me safe. They knew the dangers for young Black kids outside their front door. London (and the rest of the UK) in the '80s and '90s was a hotbed of young Black kids being disproportionally excluded from school, being arrested and jailed, being sectioned under the Mental Health Act, and having to deal with a racist Metropolitan Police force. I'll break down the numbers, to give you an idea of what immigrant parents were facing at the time.

In his research paper of 1996, Professor David Gillborn's assessment of the disparities in attainment levels according to ethnicity are stark, and he is seen as one of the first to look at the numbers properly. In the paper he shows that whenever exclusion rates were broken down by ethnicity, Black students were always over-represented. At the time, African Caribbean students were between four and six times more likely to be excluded than their white peers. Part of the issue, according to the research, was that teachers' beliefs and actions could be such that the students did not enjoy equal opportunities to succeed.[8]

Going further, a 1997 Runnymede Trust paper found that despite several investigations into the issue of Black pupils and exclusion, there was no clear policy on how to deal with that and reverse the trend.[9]

In terms of prison populations, from the mid-1980s onwards the percentage of inmates from minority backgrounds continued to increase – especially those from an African-Caribbean background. In 1985, they represented 7.97% of the prison population in England and Wales,[10] while by December 2002 this had increased to 16.66%: an increase of 51.39%, more than any other group.

These figures show what my parents and aunts and uncles were battling against in terms of their fears for their children – the trend for the thirty years up to 2002 showed that rises in the prison population as a whole went hand in hand with an increase of the proportion coming from a minority background – but most significantly from those who were Black. A Commission for Racial Equality report in 2003 highlights the fact that the over-representation of Black males in prisons had 'a significant impact on the experience of the Black male in society at large'.

My mum's job as a social worker made her well aware of the rates at which Black people were being sectioned at the time. Let's take a snapshot of those detained under the Mental Health Act in 1983: the differences when you break it down by ethnicity are jaw-dropping, even now. Detentions were over six times more likely to be of Black people than white people, 450 versus 68 per 100,000 population. If you look at the data further, the detainment of Black men was eight times more frequent than white men.[11]

The accusations that Black people chose to play victim is a trope that has permeated through particular sectors of the media and politics for generations. But the reality is that figures such as these represent a real-life fear for those immigrants who chose to stay and raise children here, only to find that their new home was a battleground in which they had to protect both themselves and their families daily.

The list of what our parents were trying to protect us from really does go on. My mum and dad didn't want to give an inch, have me take a mile, and for it to become a decision that they went on to regret and could be powerless to take back. Added to that, they bore witness to things like the Battle of Lewisham in the summer of 1977, when hundreds of the far-right National Front tried to march from New Cross to Lewisham (a distance of a mere two miles). The protestors were emboldened by the words of one of the then-leading figures in the world of the far-right, Martin Webster: 'We believe that the multi-racial society is wrong, is evil, and we want to destroy it.'[12] Thousands of counter-demonstrators turned up, causing huge clashes.

This wasn't unusual. As more and more immigrants began to put down roots in south London, the rise of the neo-Nazis meant the far-right in the area became more prolific. As a result, they chose south London as their battleground. The British National Party had its headquarters in Eltham in the late '80s and early '90s. Thanks to this, despite the beautiful utopia of cultures and colour I was being raised with in Lewisham, about five minutes' drive from my front door was where the racists had very openly set up shop (quite literally – the office was in a bookshop) and were planning to destroy my family, me, and those who looked like me. They were doing this alongside a police force who, at the time, barely concealed their collusion. The bookshop was still open and operating the day Stephen Lawrence was murdered. It wasn't closed by the council until 1995.

Let's take a moment to look at the timing of all this in terms of my parents, and them raising Black children, safely. In 1991, I was tentatively taking my first steps into the big wide world: I was getting a sliver of freedom by going to secondary school. This milestone moment would involve me being allowed to walk the streets alone, by taking the bus to and from school. A bus that would drive along the border of Eltham.

At the time they would have been aware of what was happening just up the road. The moment that bookshop opened, racist attacks in Eltham increased, and few were ever arrested. But they couldn't keep me wrapped up in cotton wool. As a parent now, I understand better the emotional and mental arithmetic they must have had to have done to figure out what was right.

They also had to deal with it closer to home, opposite our house. I was three when we moved, and the neighbour who lived a mere stone's throw opposite refused to talk to any member of the family from the moment we moved in, to the day he died. He was disgusted we'd moved onto the road, and was flabbergasted that a black couple could afford to live in the same vicinity as him. So this nasty little man ignored us all, including me. Something else that both my parents had to deal with whenever they walked out the door, and something they would have to ignore in order to take the high road and stick to their plans for the future.

In fact, it turned out that the neighbour's wife wasn't a nasty little racist. She was lovely. After his death she found her voice. In her advancing years we helped her out a lot as a family with shopping, running errands, and doing her garden.

My parents were by no means going to live their lives according to the wishes of white racists, because as awful as it may sound, they were well used to them. Plus, they had a plan for themselves and their children, one which they were absolutely going to achieve. But they needed to do that *and* protect their children. Especially in an environment where it was well known that should anything happen, the police would not protect them, or me.

Let's see where we are with this list of things they were protecting me from: they were keeping me away from the racists, trying to stop me from getting into any trouble, trying to stop me becoming too English, and also trying to stop me losing the values I'd been raised with. In the middle of all this is just me trying to live my life. I wasn't even looking to 'live my best life' – just, you know, live my life. It was hard out here in the streets of south-east London.

I felt as though I was at the top of a tower not unlike Rapunzel's, just staring at all the amazing things other people were doing that were always out of my reach. My home may have been London, but it was a home they were always protecting me from. It's weird when you think about it that way. They didn't *choose* to make the UK their home, it was foisted upon them by their parents. But *they* chose to stay and build a family, and it was a home they felt they had to shield their children from. If they wanted to achieve the dreams they had for us, if they wanted to make that move thousands of miles across the Atlantic from the home they were born in mean something, they had no other option.

I, of course, fought against their parenting decision regularly. I very rarely won, but that didn't stop me.

My first kiss happened at a small under-eighteens party locally to my school. My friend Rosemary's parents (who were Ghanaian-born) wouldn't let her go unless I was allowed to go. My parents were similarly not keen about me going at all. But after a bit of discussion, the tightening of the immigrant parents' grip was loosened ever so slightly, and Rosemary and I couldn't believe our luck. Thinking about it now – and looking at the sassiness of my own daughter Florence (currently aged four) – I suspect the constant complaining, moaning, and my adept debating skills were probably what eventually ground them down.

We were thirteen years old, and Rosemary came round after school, both of us very excited at the prospect of going to a party without our parents being present.

Rosemary was one of the coolest girls I knew at that point in my life. She was amazing at sport, so we were on most of the school sports teams together. Her singing voice was unrivalled; the ease with which she could tackle songs by the likes of Whitney Houston and Mariah Carey was unlike anything I'd witnessed outside of a church choir environment (and she's now in the West End). She had two older brothers, one of whom went to school with my cousin Marcus. And she was beautiful, and oozed confidence. Plus, as the youngest of three siblings, she knew more about the world than me, the *oldest* of three siblings. Most importantly, though, she understood the roller coaster that was being the child of immigrants – she knew how tough it could be when you're trying to navigate that in your early teens. And as one of very few Black kids in private school at that time, she understood the delicate balance of teenage life in that environment. All things I never had to explain to her. There was a level of understanding between us that never needed to be explicitly discussed. We just got it.

Back to the night of my first kiss. At that age, I was hopelessly rubbish with boys. But that was always going to happen. I hadn't been allowed to work out how my life sat alongside them. I didn't go to school with them, I wasn't allowed to socialise with them, and due to being in a private school there tended to be more posh white boys around than Black boys . . . and the white boys had little interest in girls who didn't have blonde, long flowing hair. Rosemary and I, with our blow-dried and braided hair, were never the girls of choice: the situation served to strengthen our bond. If those posh boys dared to have conversations with us it tended to be out of curiosity more than anything else. Which, of course, did little to help my confidence. But we had each other.

The night of the first kiss started like so many others, with my dad dropping us off with a list of instructions and do's and don'ts, emphasising the time that he'd return to pick us up. It was about 7 p.m. when we pulled up outside the rugby ground sports hall, the exact start time of the party. He would be returning just after 9.30 p.m.: exactly two hours *before* the party finished. In the back of the car, Rosemary turned to me, her look of mortification exactly matching mine. We were, however, well used to making do with what we had, and stepped out of the car with our bodies full of a weird mix of excitement and disappointment.

We walked into the sports hall to disco lights and a DJ playing pop songs, with a handful of kids standing nervously on the outskirts of the room. The girls whose parents *didn't* have such a tight grip arrived well after we did, and most of the cool boys arrived after that. Once we were all in position there was a lot of twirling of girls on the dancefloor to a heavy mix of pop. I say 'mix', but the kid who was DJ-ing couldn't mix tunes for toffee. I'd been raised on a diet of sound systems at my parents' friends' parties, so the bad DJ-ing was excruciating for me. However, reviewing the music choices while scrutinising the DJ was not my primary purpose for the evening, for obvious reasons. We all danced with various potential partners until we found one that clicked, and Robert and I snuck round the back of the hall and had a kiss.

Kissing a boy wasn't explicitly on the list of things my dad had told us we couldn't do. But he didn't really have to *explicitly* tell me something that is clearly, very obviously, *absolutely* against his rules. Therefore, it was absolutely, 110 per cent going to happen in my thirteenth year. Everyone else seemed to be doing it and had been regaling their friends with stories of when they'd done it and what it was like, and I was tired of just sitting and listening. My storybook entry for that milestone was blank, and I wanted in. I was tired of doing all the things I was *supposed* to do to make my parents proud. Tired of living in my Rapunzel tower and being well behaved. I wanted to experience life too.

But in all the excitement, I got the timings wrong. Thinking about it now, the time between the boys turning up, us dancing, and me having my first kiss must have only been about an hour or so ... but time had almost seemed to stand still. It felt like I'd had a whole night with these people. By the time the kiss happened I was clearly pushing my luck timing-wise. The kiss happened at almost exactly the same time my dad was due back to pick us up. We were outside, by the side of the hall, and I had one eye on the kiss while the other eye was keeping an eye on the front door of the building round the corner.

And, because that's the kind of luck I have, in the middle of the kiss I saw my dad turn up. Bang on cue. I heard him talking to Rosemary, who told him we'd be right out and that I was in the toilet. I saw him turn round, head down the stairs, and sit in the car to wait. I then ran round the outside of the building in the opposite direction and slipped in through the door. Rosemary absolutely laughed her head off. Much like Cinderella leaving the ball, we grabbed our coats, headed out the door, and jumped into the car with silent, barely contained joy at the evening's event, knowing nothing could be discussed until we were safely in the confines of my bedroom, and could debrief in hushed voices.

Unlike Cinderella though, there was no glass slipper for my mystery kisser to use to track me down (to be honest, I doubt he was that bothered). Similarly, although I had an idea of what school he was at, there was little else to go on – and so our brief kiss was just that. And I had few opportunities to repeat that night's events since the tight grip that my parents had on my social life meant chances were few and far between. Plus, the older I got, the more people started exploring sexually, and the Black girl with the tight curls was not the top of the menu in terms of what private school boys were after.

One thing this world did show me was the privilege that was afforded to those who are moneyed and white, over those who are not. Friends' parties on the Ferrier (housing) Estate down the road were frequented regularly by the local police, with Black boys manhandled into police vans without even a slight pause or hesitation from those in authority who were tasked with slapping on the cuffs. They had little interest in explanation. Conversely, the one time I was allowed to one of the posh boys' house parties, the house in question was completely trashed by the rugby team who were at the time drunk and stoned. Cupboards doors were ripped from their hinges, fists punched into internal doors, beer and wine spilled everywhere, fag-ends left to smoulder into the expensive looking carpets. Thankfully my dad's early-exit rules still applied – he was outside in the car waiting for me long before the clock struck midnight, when the party was in full swing. But that night no arrests were made, despite the damage and the noise, the drugs and the underage drinking. It was, like so many other instances, an education in how different the life of the privileged was.

It was a world away from my Caribbean bubble that I had been used to. And I had to learn fast how to navigate it, while being raised by Jamaican parents determined to ensure I wasn't enamoured by it. Parents who also wanted to make sure I never forgot who I was, so their tight grip, although it slightly lessened over time, was still firmly there. It meant that I could merely glance into that world, never fully be a part of it. Not that the boys in that world would have completely accepted me at that time, anyway. A lot of it was based on looks, privilege, and wealth. I was Black, so less attractive to them, I had no privilege, and my family was firmly working class. There was no benefit to them to have me in their world.

I didn't need to pretend I was something I wasn't in that beautiful microcosm of British Caribbean culture – I could just be me. But even with that, as I got older and more confident, things became more difficult. I spoke differently than the kids who were out shopping with their mums in Lewisham Market, the kids I hung out with at church, and even most of my cousins. Not only did I stand out among the white private school kids you'd see at various sporting events, or socially . . . I was beginning to stand out among the very group that gave me solace. Most didn't say anything about it, and treated me exactly the same. To some, though, the changes in my voice and my confidence levels were seen as me turning my back on my Blackness. As if I'd somehow scraped the Black off my skin with a putty knife and was showing the white girl inside. Internalised racism has a long history.

My mum and aunt's Caribbean twang coupled with their immigrant status meant that secondary school was hard for them. My aunt was in the British education system from 1962–71. By 1964, the children of migrants made up 2 per cent of the school population, two-thirds of whom were of Caribbean origin – and from the beginning, the clash between the system and immigrants were evident. This despite the fact that the children had been raised in Jamaica on a system that was modelled on the British education system with a very similar syllabus. One could argue, then, that it should have been a fairly simple and swift transition. And yet it wasn't. They were mostly placed in inner-city schools which were already struggling, with teachers who struggled to understand the dialect, and didn't try. Teachers who continually decided the label 'immigrant' translated to 'lacking intelligence', resulting in the normal run-of-the-mill racism and prejudice.

From the side of immigrant parents, they had come from communities where a good education was paramount. But they would come not from huge schools in Jamaica, but smaller communities with smaller classes, and a smaller school environment which would encourage constant interaction with teachers, and a high level of trust between teacher and parent. In post-war Britain with its large school institutions, and, again, its run-of-the-mill racism and prejudice, what my grandparents *thought* they were going to get out of the British education system for their children, and what they actually got, were two very different things.

Once again, if the assumption hadn't been that these kids were stupid, imagine the impact it would have had economically had these kids been given the education they deserved. By the end of the 1960s, Black British children were entering the labour market, and it became evident, especially with Black British boys, that many were doing so without the appropriate qualifications which in turn increased their chances of being unemployed. A cycle which, for some, became never-ending.

But by the mid-1960s, almost predictably, the presence of *all* migrant children in schools became a hot topic over fears they weren't integrating properly. As a result, eleven local authorities decided there should be no more than 30 per cent of immigrants in any one school (pick a number, any number), and once that quota was reached the children were taken elsewhere. Although this isn't a situation that applied to my aunt and mum's local area, it gives a taste of what kind of battle immigrant children were caught in the middle of. Integration as a two-way street was an alien concept.[13]

Although Black kids were not always being bussed out, they had other political issues hanging over their heads to keep them in line: special schools. Children of the Windrush generation were being disproportionately downgraded in the system as being 'Educationally Subnormal' (ESN) and sent away to specialist schools. The decision was often made by using IQ tests which were biased. The children in question were labelled as 'backward', 'slow' or 'a dunce', but the special schools they ended up at were anything but: the schools had no curriculum, no exams, and no qualifications. Unsurprisingly, the impact of being sent to them would be felt for a lifetime in terms of, among other things, life chances and employment. A leaked report from the Inner London Education Authority later revealed that, yes, the ESN's decisions were being applied disproportionately to Black children.[14]

This is the environment my mum and my aunts on both sides of my family were being educated in. A system that was desperate to label them as stupid and send them away, a system that believed segregation was the key to integration. A system that seemed hell-bent on ensuring that those of a darker hue understood that their position in life deserved to get no higher, and the British education system was going to ensure that happened. Through the '70s and '80s though, the situation became better. Not perfect, but better. However, some disparities still existed.

But in the 1980s when my mum and aunts' careers were in full swing, and they had school-aged children themselves, they made key decisions about what they wanted to do about those disparities: my mum chose to work in mental health and with children and families, while my aunt became a teacher and later a deputy head. Both wanted to ensure the next generation had a bit more support from within the system.

In terms of education for their kid, how I spoke was a big part of that. Which is understandable, considering the impact their dialect had in a racist education system. So, out was the south-east London twang, and in came regular elocution and drama lessons in my younger years so that I would learn to talk, as they saw it, 'properly'. What they hadn't taken into account is the impact that would then have. Yes, it meant that I spoke with confidence at school, and my perfectly pitched English accent and pronunciation meant that my voice stood out less. I was the only Black kid in primary school anyway, so I was always going to stand out, but they just wanted to give me a helping hand.

Rather than a voice that was a hybrid of Jamaica and London, I began pronouncing my T's, and stopped dropping vowels. Interestingly, it took until my adulthood to stop pronouncing H as 'H-aitch', and I still find it difficult to say 'asked' rather than 'arksed'. No amount of elocution lessons could completely take the Jamaican out of me. Lol.

What the elocution and the private school environment did teach me from an early age was how to successfully change my behaviour in order to make myself appear more palatable to the majority in professional environments. This phenomenon is now known in modern parlance as 'code switching': the ways in which an underrepresented group consciously or unconsciously adjusts their language, syntax, and grammatical structure, behaviour, and appearance to fit into the dominant culture. A definition which can sum up so many of our lives as adults, but I spent most of my childhood doing exactly that, straddling those worlds. I realise now, as an adult, how exhausting that was.

When I've watched my elders do it in both professional and church environments, for that matter, it's something that colloquially in Jamaican patois we call 'speaky spokey': to affect a non-local accent and speech mannerisms. This is how so many lose the Jamaican lilt in their sentence constructions, diction, structure and syntax. The longer they use the 'foreign' tongue in order to fit in and stop it being used as a racist and ignorant stick to beat them with, the more likely they are to lose to ability to use their 'mother' tongue. My mum eventually lost her accent, my dad kept his. My guess is that going to school here and working in an office environment was why my mum lost hers; my dad conversely worked for himself for many years. But those still able to effectively shapeshift between Caribbean and English should be winning Best Actor Oscars on a daily basis.

Losing most of my Jamaica-London hybrid sound opened up a hornet's nest that didn't really stop completely biting me in the arse until adulthood. If it wasn't a handful of Black kids calling me a coconut on the bus or at house parties in my late teens, it was extended family members consistently mimicking my voice and gaining joy from talking disparagingly about how I sounded every single time they stepped into our house. I didn't have the words as a kid to really convey how much it hurt. Although I didn't have the effective vocabulary to really express how it impacted me, the feeling sat firmly on my heart. And it hurt, a lot. Every part of me was Jamaican. I was raised in a Jamaican household, most of my life was spent around those of Caribbean heritage. I was living in this Caribbean microcosm when I wasn't at school ... I hadn't even, by this point in my life, eaten proper British food. I was a Jamaican growing up in Britain.

And yet to some, the way I spoke meant all of that just faded away.

'Internalised racism' is a formal definition that has had a relatively short lifespan. Back when I was younger, there wasn't a definition, or an understanding that you could be racist to your own. You just accepted it was what it was. And for years it felt as though I was balancing between the person I knew I was in the place that felt most akin to the person I was raised to be, and how others perceived me and where they *thought* I should be.

But it didn't make me turn away from this beautiful microcosm of Caribbean culture, because it was still a lifeline. The culture with which I was raised made me who I am. Yes, I am British born and bred – and yet I'm reminded regularly that this fact doesn't necessarily mean I'm equal. Even on the most basic level, I may be able to walk down to the local high street and find a shop selling products for my hair. But I still can't walk into any hairdressers anywhere in the country and get my hair washed and blow-dried – because to most hairdressers my type of hair is a mystery they can't be bothered to solve or get training in. But if you have Caucasian hair and require a blow-dry? Any Afro hairdressers will sit you in their chair and do it without hesitation or worry. Compare that to the panicked faces that greet me when I walk into a Caucasian hairdressers. The way in which the minority seamlessly adjusts itself to successfully fit into the majority continues. Hairdressing students learning about Afro hair only became a mandatory part of cutting and styling training in 2020. In other words, students will have to work with Black hair in order to become a qualified hairdresser.

But there does reach a point when you tire of fighting to be accepted on a level playing field in a country where you are a minority, and just want to ... exist. And for those of my parents' generation there are many who decided to move back to Jamaica in the final chapter of their lives – a country that stayed in their hearts for ever, and to which they have consistently planned to move back to.

That feeling I get when I step off the plane in Jamaica, that overwhelming sense of joy, is multiplied tenfold for my parents – and for many of their contemporaries. Unlike me, where it *feels* like home, for them, it *was* home. That feeling is like the tiniest of threads that remain intact over the decades: connecting you to the country of your birth. For some that thread wears out over time, and the yearning diminishing year after year. But for others it tugs constantly, sometimes softly, sometimes with an overwhelming urgency. It reminds you that no matter how much the UK can make you feel rejected, despondent, and like you don't matter ... that there is another way. That you have the most beautiful get-out clause, the ability to grab tight on that thread and for it to pull you 'home'. A theme that's been repeated by immigrants from the world over who've moved to the UK. Not all, but some.

I don't remember a time as a child or an adult where my dad's yearning ever stopped. As far back as I can remember, the plan was to go back to the Jamaica in retirement. The UK may have become his home in his late teens, but his connection to the country of his birth never waned. It's interesting when you talk to those who don't have immigrant parents, whose parents are around regularly – they do find it curious that my dad lives so far away for half the year. For me, it's as it was always meant to be. Knowing how much he sacrificed and worked in *this* home, his other home ... he deserves to be able to live out his final chapter in the home that's been part of his plan since he left.

The same applies to my uncle Errol. He was born in Jamaica and moved to the UK in his mid-teens and joined the British Army, being stationed in bases the world over. In his later years, he hotfooted it back to Jamaica upon his retirement, a plan which had been in the works as long as I can remember. Unlike my dad, who waited a few years after retirement before he left, my uncle flew off sharpish. The swiftness with which he upped and left made us all chuckle. When I visited him once and asked him why this need to leave never left him; his answer perfectly encapsulated the reasons there are so many 'returnees', irrespective of which country you're going back to: 'Britain was the land of opportunity, Jamaica was in my heart.'

My uncle has always had a way with words, but it's a sentence that has never left me. The beauty with which those few words reflect the true nature of the immigrant experience fills me with such joy. He has two homes, each where he fulfilled a specific stage in his life and I have a huge amount of respect for that decision.

My uncle has always been an important figure for our whole family – I love and miss him dearly. However, each time I visit him in the years since he departed the UK, never to return, I see the impact being 'home' has on him, the same as I did with my grandad before his death. My uncle has always been the one who looks most similar to my grandad, so the physical impact of being back in Jamaica was visible in the same ways – despite them being decades apart. Their bodies looked less heavy, their skin looked healthy and glowing, their smiles seemed brighter. Every part of their being just seemed lighter.

Yes, there's the obvious impact of retiring from the daily grind of work, but that wasn't the sum total of the joy. It also comes from being back in the place that holds your heart. As much as both my uncle and grandad raised families in the UK, it never completely had their hearts. When there is so much that consistently tells you that you don't belong, when you're never truly accepted for who you are and what you look like, joy can come from just *being* without explanation. And for my uncle and grandad, Jamaica brought that joy to their hearts. The armour they had to drag onto their weary bodies once the reality of UK life hit home instantly disintegrated over the Atlantic as they made their final journeys home. Being able to be culturally free? To be able to let the tension that you've held in those shoulders for so long finally ease? The beauty of that cannot be underestimated.

I finally returned to Jamaica, for the first time since Covid, in 2023. It was a big family holiday involving younger cousins, older cousins, partners, siblings, and aunts. For my cousin and I, making sure our children have a connection to Jamaica is important. We're the same age, with the exact same experiences of being raised in a Jamaican household in London. The culture made us who we are, and the thought of losing that connection would be heartbreaking for both of us. We both still have family in Jamaica, and we both understand the importance of having our children see where and how their various grandparents were raised. A connection to your roots is important, especially as you get older. In much the same way that we are the sum of two cultures, so are our children. Our passports say British, but our hearts and experiences are a sum of both. My cousin's boys are older than my two children, so seeing their joy at finally seeing the country they had been told so much about was something special that we'll remember for ever, I think.

Purely by chance, the Jamaican dancehall legend Beenie Man was on our flight, and during the stopover he wandered up and down the aisles chatting to the other passengers and giving a couple of impromptu performances. Tourists with little to no knowledge of the culture were clueless about what was causing such a level of excitement during a two-hour stopover on a plane in the Bahamas. The rest of us couldn't believe we were singing 'Sim Simma Who Got The Keys To My Bimma' loudly on a Virgin flight alongside the King of Dancehall. It was the obvious, loud reaction to discovering a Jamaican superstar on your flight. The British reaction would have been slightly subdued, but the Jamaican reaction was loudly clapping and singing along with him. We don't need booze to lose our inhibitions – Jamaicans can be loud and raucous without any need for lubrication … we can be stone-cold sober, screaming the lyrics to 'Gyal Dem Sugar' on the 11.30 a.m. Virgin flight from London Heathrow. My gosh, I love us.

During the trip we travelled to see my aunt in Brown's Town, St Anns. She was the aunt who had the agreement with my parents to fly to the UK once they knew that my mum was in her final weeks of life. She then stayed with us for months after my mum's death, helping us with our transition from a four-person family, to three. Her presence in our house during what was one of the darkest and most distressing moments in our lives will be etched in my heart for ever. She left her family and children in Jamaica to help look after ours. Because that's how family works. I constantly wished that she'd never leave; having this bossy Jamaican in our house brought such comfort. Our house smelt of Jamaica every day she was there. She was always cooking one of our favourite Jamaican dishes: fried dumpling, plantain, ackee and saltfish, gizzadas, roast pork, fried chicken, curry goat, curry chicken. It was the most Jamaican our house had smelt in quite some time because of mum's declining health. Food had understandably taken a back seat.

Even writing this now is making me a bit emotional, which has surprised me. Maybe because I've realised it really was the final time our house smelt so Jamaican. As well as my aunt's cooking, there was a constant stream of aunties (real and acquired) who would bring pots and pots of curries, and tray upon tray of fried chicken and fish. It was quite a sight to behold. Our house was so full of people every day the food needed replenishing constantly, yet we never seemed to run out.

Waking up to Aunty Annette's fried dumpling, ackee and saltfish and hard food, seasoned in a way that meant it was quintessentially her food, made me so happy. I'm not sure if I can explain it properly, but the Jamaican matriarch in our home was slowly but surely leaving us. The woman who was one half of the couple that made our home a small slice of Jamaica in south-east London. And I was so scared to lose that. But with Aunty Annette we could hold onto that for a little bit longer. Our house could smell of Jamaica a little bit longer. Afterwards, my dad was brilliant at taking over the cooking mantle, with me holding up the rear, but it was different. The kitchen felt quieter. Without mum it felt like a small slice of our Jamaican home was gone.

Visits to my Aunty Annette in Jamaica mean the world to me and my siblings. It's a house we've frequented many times over the years, from when we were young children. So it's as though for a brief moment in time we get those memories back. Her house hasn't changed at all in my entire life. Yes, a couple bits of furniture have been updated over the years, and they built a small apartment for visitors at the end of the yard – but essentially the only home I have memories of that haven't changed is at Aunty Annette and Uncle Mike's house. Various other family members have sold their homes, passed away, had renovations, or downsized. I could make my way around Aunty Annette's place blindfolded and not bump into a thing. It's the only home that I can say that about. The time I've spent in that house is immeasurable. So being able to take my kids there to be with her is a big thing for me. It's the place where I can tell them, 'I grew up here!' and can share memories of every room they walk into. It's worlds apart from the home they grow up in, in London, but is also full of so much love.

It a higgledy-piggledy house, with what used to be my aunt's hairdressing salon in the basement. It sits opposite two vacant lots of land, one which takes a huge drop down a steep hill. The other is the graveyard of a disused church, currently housing someone rearing goats. But compared to the other parts of Brown's Town, it's fairly chill. All you'd mostly hear is people yelling up to the veranda for whichever Schleiffer the individual was after, be that my cousins, my uncle, or my aunt. Whole conversations would be had while we sat on that veranda: my aunt yelling to the pavement below, the visitor yelling up to her. That's just how they rolled. Not much had changed when we visited the summer of 2023, much to the amusement of my children who, in London, are constantly told to stop shouting.

And, predictably, I revert back to Jamaican mode when I visit. We pulled up in Uncle Errol's car, I got to the gate at the bottom of the steps and yelled, 'Mrs Schleiffer!' No response. 'Mrs Schleiffer!' Again no response. So I dig deep for the emergency yell, 'Ah-nnette!' Finally my beautiful aunty came into view from the kitchen door, with a face that age clearly continues to run away from. She always looks exactly the same, no matter the time that has passed between us. Glasses on, hair slicked back, in a top and long skirt as ever.

'But Charlene, I thought it was a Jamaican shouting for me!'

'Why, thank you,' I replied, pretending to bow, and killing myself laughing. It's incredible how the elocution lessons tend to automatically take a back seat once I'm with the family in Jamaica.

Once I'd made sure the vicious dogs had been locked away, with only the nice ones left to wander the yard, I left the kids with my brother and his girlfriend to make their way up the stairs and I just ran to my aunt for the biggest, longest hug. Now that my grandad has passed, she is the one that means 'home' to me. Not just because of her presence in my house when my mum passed, but because she and her children, my cousins, have been my connection to Jamaica for my entire life: she didn't leave to live in the UK, she stayed and raised a family. So if Jamaica can feel like home, sitting high up on the stools in Aunty Annette's kitchen chatting while she cooks is the place I feel most at home there. It's a scene that has been repeated time and time again throughout my life. From my dad lifting me onto those stools, to me being tall enough to reach them myself. Helping my kids – aged three and six years old in the summer of 2023 – onto those stools had the familiarity of someone who'd been making those exact moves on autopilot their whole life, on those exact stools. My bottom on those stools fit like feet into a familiar pair of shoes – they're as hard as anything, and possibly the most uncomfortable stools ever for long stints. But they have unrivalled familiarity for my bottom, which means it can sit on it for hours perfectly, changing from cheek to cheek when one becomes numb. My aunty does have a dining table and chairs in the other room, but I genuinely can't remember a time in history when I've actually sat at that table.

My brother and his girlfriend sat at it that day due to so many of us being in the house and not enough stools, and I absolutely promise you that I stared at them in awe when they sat down at it for dinner. Like, what on earth are you doing, bruh?! Seeing the kitchen/diner from that vantage point was, and still is, a complete unknown to me, and I'm too old for change: it would feel weird. *And* there's an old-school, American-style kitchen hatch between the kitchen and the dining room, and because 'my' seat at the counter is on the corner it meant I either had to completely ignore my brother and his girlfriend over dinner, or talk to them through the wall behind me. I absolutely refuse to sit on any other stool to eat. It makes me feel discombobulated. So I chose to converse with them once they'd come to their senses and stood up to eat.

My aunty spoils us. She always has. As does my Aunty Eleanor in the UK. We don't have grandparents around to spoil us any more. So getting that from my aunts, especially in Jamaica, makes me revert back to being a kid. She refuses to let us help prepare food, she refuses to have us help her clear up. She gets to see us so infrequently she just wants us to be present in the moment, and I'll be thankful for those moments for ever.

She's also aware that being *truly* present in the moment can only be fully achieved if she cooks us a selection of our favourite things. On our 2023 visit, there was fried fish (my brother's favourite), spicy roast pork, fried chicken in barbecue sauce (my favourites) then all the required essential sides – my aunt's famous cabbage salad, rice and peas, and macaroni cheese. No jerk though: my aunt has consistently refused to cook jerk anything – she's never been a fan of that particular collection of spices. And I have learnt to forgive her for that, over time.

It was hot that summer, hotter than summers past. The

effect of climate change caused by nations far away. As the sun beat harshly into the kitchen, muscle memory had me leaning back to flick on the fan which has also never moved location. There's a reason *why* this stool has always been my favourite. My mother never raised no fool.

To those who don't have immigrant parents, the peaceful familiarity that can come from sitting in a kitchen miles away from home – in a culture far removed from so-called 'British culture' – can be difficult to get your head around. It's not a holiday location that you return to, or a random holiday house, it's not a B&B that you visit every year, it *is* home for me. An extension of the Jamaican household I grew up in, in London. That is why my mum chose her cousin, my Aunty Annette, to help us with transitioning from her death.

The memories of running around this place with my plentiful cousins fill my soul. Sitting downstairs in my aunt's salon while she rescued my hair from the overuse of products in the UK, while she yelled at me for not being careful enough with what I let those 'English hairdressers' put on my hair, will always make me chuckle. My aunt's hands haven't been in my hair for years now (motherhood means I usually braid it when I visit now. I have no time for haircare, two kids, and the humidity of Jamaica), but even when she was roughly putting a comb through it and laughing as I struggled under a steamer in the middle of the sort of summer heat that was definitely alien to me, I'll always connect those moments with the endless love that she had for us. The love that constantly radiates from her, and the obvious love that she has for us means that it doesn't matter if we only see her in person every four years . . . the love we have for each other never diminishes. And that is the definition of family.

Despite the relentless cussing about me not calling her enough, our afternoon together was over. My belly was definitely full, and my heart even more so. But the moment we started driving away, I missed her. I missed her love, I missed her presence, I just missed who I was when I was with her. Not a parent, not a TV presenter, not a journalist ... just the niece that gets spoilt every time she walks through her door. The niece who, the moment she drives through Brown's Town past the huge market on the left, and the sweet shop on the right by the roundabout – is transported back to the Jamaican home she grew up visiting.

I don't feel like I *have* to decide where I call home but it's an interesting debate to have – especially if you are an immigrant family. That thread was ever present for my uncle, parents and grandparents, becoming more pronounced, its emotional pull becoming more urgent, in their advancing years. It's as though the call, a faint whisper when they disembarked that plane when they first arrived, began yelling louder and louder until they could no longer ignore it. And so they packed up and headed out.

That thread, although so clear in the minds of some members of my family, does not tug as strongly with me. I don't feel like I'm alone in that, I suspect it's a feeling experienced by most of us who are first-generation born somewhere else. My emotional pull to Jamaica isn't quite as simple as it is for them. My connection to the place of their birth is undeniable, but my urge to be there is more complex and nuanced: it's an amalgamation of so many different things rolled into one. I remember talking to writer-director Adjani Salmon about just this, during the release of his TV series *Dreaming While Black*. Having spent most of his childhood in Jamaica, he didn't experience or understand what racism was until he moved back to the UK as an adult, and got a taste of it first-hand. He learnt what it was to be Black from the perspective of those who were not.

In Jamaica I do not have to be 'unapologetically Black', I'm just, well, Black. I don't have to do the physical and mental gymnastics required in order to mould myself into something more palatable for the majority. I can just be me. When the immigration officer at Sangster International Airport in Montego Bay says, 'Welcome home' to me when he stamps my passport, a wave of belonging passes over me. Which always shocks me as it hits.

After a lifetime of being the jigsaw piece that doesn't quite completely fit into the puzzle of British life, you become accustomed to a particular version of yourself. You're used to that ever-present suit of armour that's ready to leap into action when an off-the-cuff, low-level racist remark is thrown in your direction, with the aim of reminding you to know your place. A reminder, perhaps, that you don't completely belong in this home. The older I get, the more I understand why my parents raised me the way they did. Growing up in a Jamaican household in London protected me from what was beyond those walls for a little bit longer. It helped to preserve my innocence to the harsh reality of being a Black woman growing up as a minority here. If I mostly grew up in the community, I could, perhaps gain strength from that and take time to build my armour. And it worked. That is why there will always be room in my heart for each of my 'homes'. It's not rejecting my Britishness or diminishing my Jamaican heritage. There is space for both.

Much like Jamaica, Britain is a nation based on its multicultural roots, however distasteful that may seem to others. The creation of the British Empire in the late 1500s aided the creation of those roots, and yet some five hundred years later it still has an unbalanced relationship with it. But compare that to Jamaica, which has sitting under its coat of arms, the English motto: 'Out of Many, One People'. A celebration, then, of the multicultural tapestry from which the nation was created.

Conversely, sitting under the UK's coat of arms is its motto: 'Dieu et mon droit'. Translated from French, it means, 'God and my right'. Two very clear and distinctly different mottos, with wildly different sentiments. One of my homes wholeheartedly accepts what it is, whereas my other home has had a near five-hundred-year fight with itself about what it is. It's crazy. But it's a duality that so many immigrants have lived with for ever.

Chapter 2

Growing Up in Care

When you take nostalgia and heart out of the equation, the place you feel safe and secure has a big part to do with where you feel most at home. Whatever else is happening outside in the world, when you put the key in the door of your home all of that is supposed to slip away: the place you call home – wherever that may be – is supposed to envelop you, hug you, slow the beating of a tense and anxious heart. It's supposed to bring you joy, yes. But it's also the place that you're supposed to feel safe. To have that every day really is a privilege that many of us take for granted. It didn't matter how hard things became financially for my family – especially after the 1993 financial crash – I grew up in a house where we'd get meals three times a day, where cuddles were always available, and where, when my head hit that pillow at night, I could sleep soundly, then wake with a mind purely focused on the day ahead. Of course, there were days where I'd wake with dread, having had a massive telling-off the night before for some mischievous act that had rendered me grounded. But I was never scared of home.

Whatever battle my parents were fighting in the world out-side, be that to do with work or finances, they never brought it home to us. They, like many parents, threw a protective blanket around our home to protect us from what was beyond our walls. It wasn't a utopia of course; my younger sister and I could bicker and scream at each other in a way that could rival any episode of *The Bold and the Beautiful*. My parents insistence on discipline being high on the agenda meant that they could be harsh, and at times incredibly unfair with their tellings-off. My mum, though I obviously loved her deeply, could be insensitive and the top end of annoying at times. All things which were, I would argue, run-of-the-mill when it came to the dynamics of a family household.

Was I aware that others didn't grow up in the same way? Unlike most of my friends, yes I was. As I became older, my mum became more honest about the work that she did – and the dark lives that kids my age had to try to survive in. I sus-pect it was her way of making me understand how the life that they'd created for us compared to those who were not so lucky. And it worked. I was raised knowing that for some kids, walking through the front door of their home didn't calm the beating of a heart, it quickened it. And that the scraping sound of a key beginning its journey into the hole of a door, then turning and releasing the lock, could instil fear and dread before the door was even pushed open. I was very aware of that from the moment I turned thirteen. I guess my mum thought I was old enough at that point to understand the reality of 'real life' outside the walls of our house on Pitfold Road.

Now that I'm a parent, I can understand why she switched

from the Children and Families division at Lewisham Council, to the division that worked with the elderly in the last few years of her life. She was a mum of three, and at some point it just becomes too hard emotionally to have your own children while constantly doing your best to help the children of others process extreme levels of abuse, degradation and trauma. All of which took place in their own homes. I remember her becoming very uncomfortable with us sitting on our uncles' laps at family events, not because she genuinely thought anything would happen, but because the cases began to consume her, and she began to see every older male family member in our home as a potential predator. The only way she could deal with that was to make sure that we were never left in any situations that could be misconstrued – or become dangerous. Leaving the division probably saved her sanity.

But what it left me with was a level of understanding of how our home life compared to others. I knew that I was blessed and privileged to have grown up in my home. The laughter and noise that would fill every nook and cranny of the house from top to bottom at family gatherings and barbecues; the anxious silence that would fill it when mum was in hospital having treatment; the sounds of a bunch of screaming children running around like headless chickens at one of our birthday parties. I rewatched a video of my seventh birthday party recently and, aside from the fact we videoed way too much content when we hired VHS camcorders back in the day, seeing all that joy and love in our house just had me grinning so much I couldn't stop. My parents had invited the whole class (it was a small school luckily!), my cousins, aunts and uncles – so the house was packed. Their good friend, my

Uncle George, was there too, and it turned out that despite not *actually* being a kids' entertainer he was great at it. He spent two hours playing party games with all the kids, and making up silly dancing challenges. He made that party, and the stage was set for summer birthday parties year after year afterwards. And they remain some of my strongest memories.

I rewatched the video because I was reminded about how much you can take your home life for granted after a conversation with the foster care campaigner and consultant Chris Wild. A safe and secure home should be the norm, but for so many kids it's not. And yet for Chris and me the first ten years of our lives were very similar, the normality of that life and that security shining so brightly in both our lives.

'I always say it was a very normal upbringing. We were a very normal Yorkshire working-class family. We went on holiday once a year. We lived in a little community where in the summertime everybody was out in the street playing football. Everyone had a mum and a dad; there was nobody whose parents were divorced or who'd lost a parent.' He smiles as he says this, reliving the memory of his childhood in a house full of love.

He grew up with a house with his mum and dad and older sister, in Halifax in Yorkshire. His grandma was an immigrant (of sorts) like mine, moving to England from Northern Ireland when she was young, to a country that was less than welcoming to the Irish. 'She really struggled. She had a really tough life coming from Northern Ireland to Halifax; they weren't accepted. So they build their own little communities. Grandma was really stoic, and she had this resilience about her.'

There are similarities between Caribbean and Irish families, with the grandparents' home being the centre and the insistence on family being together at all times, especially for big occasions and celebrations. Much like the key memories in my life at that time, Christmas morning and the rest of Christmas Day is etched in both of our minds. 'I remember waking up and getting my brand-new tracksuit on, and the day was really colourful and magical.' Much like me, his parents were like the embodiment of a grown-up pulling a child into a hug towards their chest, holding them tightly so that they can't peek out to see any of the bad stuff: an iron-clad ring, softened by love. 'You didn't see any evil or you didn't even know bad things happened in the world because you were protected from that. Grandma was in the centre of that.' His grandad was known to take himself away from the madness in the kitchen and seek solace and no doubt peace in front of the television, 'He was quite an intellect, my grandad. He'd take himself off to watch the news. He could watch television twenty-four hours a day. He could be cantankerous. But he was still there.'

Chris's memory of being surrounded by family – parents, grandparents, uncles, aunts and cousins – while beans, bacon and eggs were fried in his grandma's kitchen on Christmas morning does sound idyllic; in fact, he just calls it, 'a magical morning. Really, really magical.'

Christmas lunch would then be back home, with his dad cooking up a storm in their kitchen, serving a meal for them all to devour. His dad grew up in foster care and was homeless and living on the streets at sixteen years old, so he wanted to create the home for his children that he was not lucky enough to have himself. The father that Chris calls 'my hero' is the man that to this day Chris is trying his best to emulate. 'He was really loved. And he was really gentle. He was kind. He was courteous, didn't have a bad bone in his body. If you were to bring any danger to the family, he was the protector as well, because his family was everything to him. We were just infused with love.' He paused at this point, taking a breath. 'He wanted to protect us from that world, that different world that he knew growing up, the world we didn't even know existed.'

That's the bubble that is sometimes underestimated by those of us who were privileged enough to grow up with a home life like Chris. Although it may not seem like it at the time (hindsight is a wonderful thing), living in a Disney-esque bubble of protection is what helps us to keep our youth and innocence. *That* is the essence of a childhood home, and the responsibility of parenting, I guess. No matter what is going on outside those walls of a home, you try to protect your child from the worst of it. Love and protection are the undeniable base ingredients of the place a kid can call home. It's their sanctuary of sorts. That's something you may not always understand as a child, but it's when you hit adulthood – and especially parenthood – that you realise that it's an essential part of a functioning childhood experience.

Which is why when Chris tell me, 'We had stability. We had love. Every morning he'd make an effort to pick me up and say: "I love you, I love you,"' it breaks my heart, because the pain that came next in his life seems unfathomable compared to the bliss that went before.

Chris' life chimes with me because we are only about

seven months apart in age, meaning that at eleven years old, we were both in our final year of primary school, with the frissons of excitement beginning to stir in our heads at the thought of heading to secondary school. He may have been miles away in Halifax and me in London, but the sentiment was the same: we were both on the cusp of a new adventure, and a new chapter in the story of our childhoods. And then, through no fault of our own, fate placed us on different paths. Mine continued with the love and security within the four walls of my home, but for Chris something inexplicably shifted in the universe and started turning the brightness in his life down, dimming the lights ... until eventually the switch that controlled the light and love and joy was abruptly and cruelly turned off.

I was still being shielded by a grown-up hug of protection at home, sheltering me from the bad in the world. But for Chris, without warning, the arms of protection suddenly and simply fell away. Just like that: no preamble, no preparation, no adjustment period. With a flick of a switch it all just disappeared. At eleven years old, his dad passed away, which triggered a domino effect that would change the course of his life for ever, and which he would spend his life trying to recover from.

His dad, due to a weak immune system after a childhood of being passed around in foster care, caught chicken pox from Chris's sister during the Autumn of 1990. By the spring, he was in hospital and on life support, with shingles having taken over his body. He died on April Fool's Day 1991. The heart of Chris's home, the centre of his family's life, was gone, and the effect on all of them was instantaneous. 'I remember my mum having a breakdown and grandma hugging her like a mother would. And I saw all that security, all that love, just dismantle within a second of that phone call.'

Having lived in a home full of love, it was incomprehensible that it could disappear. 'You think it's just a moment, that it's going to pass. I remember being really silent and thinking, 'When is this moment going to end?' It didn't. And as the days went on everything crumbled, the foundation just crumbled.'

He pauses and looks away, the memory of what was lost still weighing very heavily on his heart. 'It was like going from a really colourful movie like *The Wizard of Oz* to something really dark and melancholic in black and white. Everything went grey. It was like a nebulous cloud.'

Trying to navigate his way through the fog proved fruitless. Losing the centre of the home left his entire family off-balance and discombobulated. No one seemed to know *how* to keep the home on an even keel when its centre had been ripped away. 'I remember it vividly. Grandma became so isolated; this really stoic woman became really cold. The whole community just stopped. I think they didn't know how to approach it; they didn't understand it. So, the whole community alienated us. We stopped getting invited around to people's houses very quickly, because Dad wasn't there. At school, the kids didn't know how to approach me. So, then I became really cold and lonely and isolated.'

His mum, neither able to process her grief or step into the shoes of the man who was the heart of their home, turned to alcohol. 'Mum would be crying and go upstairs. And his clothes were still in the wardrobe, and the scent of him was still there. But he wasn't there. And that's how it just dissolved. It became so dysfunctional very quickly. Mum started drinking until she was unconscious. Within two months of my dad dying, I'd come home to her unconscious.'

At eleven years old, Chris didn't have the capacity to navigate a world without his dad, and with a mum who was unable to reach out beyond her own loss to help Chris with his. 'It's a really strange feeling that you can never get over. And you think maybe *this* is the dream, and I'm still asleep somewhere. That's how it feels as an eleven-year-old. Your hero is gone. It's like having all your limbs removed. It's really difficult to articulate because it's subjective to other people. But for me it was a nightmare. Like something I desperately wanted to wake up from.'

These traumatic events triggered the next step of the domino effect, with Chris consistently getting himself into trouble. But the trivial things he was doing, like shoplifting from Woolworths or stealing sweets from the local sweetshop, was nothing, truly nothing compared to the magnitude of what happened next. The safety net of home, which was already diminishing, was pulled from underneath him. 'Everything was taken away', he says. The police had brought him home one too many times to his mum passed out unconscious from booze and decided enough was enough. The decision was made to take him to the now-infamous Skircoat Lodge Children's Home in Halifax.

When Chris found out he was excited, and the reason for the excitement is heartbreaking. Because a children's home has the word 'home' in it, he assumed he was being taken somewhere that would allow him to get back the light that had been lost after his dad died. He thought the black-and-white film that his life had become was on the verge of getting its colour back. 'I thought it was going to be like a theme park holiday or something, like Butlins.' And so he packed his bag for his new home.

Chris turned twelve just before he was moved to his new home, and it's interesting to think about what you may well pack to take with you at that stage of your life. As a grown-up you think more saliently and maturely about the things that are important to you. But I don't think Chris did too badly: he brought jewellery that belonged to his dad, a chain, so that he felt close to him, and the basics that any kid his age would find essential, the specificity of the list perhaps an adult-reflection of the magnitude of the act of packing for what turned out to be the final journey he'd take as a child from the only home he'd ever known. 'I had a little Umbro bag, it was blue. And I remember putting my boxer shorts in there. I was getting to that age where I was wearing boxer shorts and underpants. I remember that because the transition [happens at around] eleven to twelve years old.' Added to his blue Umbro bag were things like a couple of T-shirts, a couple of pairs of jeans and a couple of pairs of trainers.

As excitement kept growing in anticipation of moving to his new home, 'I was thinking this is great, somebody's going to help me. Somebody's going to take this pain away. I can be somewhere where I don't have to either protect Mum any more or be subjected to this kind of abuse where Mum was just constantly drunk and unconscious or in pain every hour of the day.'

I really wish that had been the case. The warmth and

calmness you feel when you meet Chris belies the chaos that ensued the moment he walked out of his childhood home and got in that car to Skircoat Lodge. The drive up the hill to the children's home was picture-perfect, he says, and the buildings and the grounds were 'picturesque' with old Yorkshire stone surrounded by tall trees; he describes it as almost *Downton Abbey*-esque. He talks of the car snaking its way past the trees on the way up to the main building where the entrance was. He explains the location in great detail, possibly because it was the final normal experience he had before his world became even darker. 'It was what I call a mild spring in Halifax, where the sun's there and it has that essence of a summer. You can smell it. It had a quietness, a beautiful quietness. Because you're not in Halifax's town centre, you're quite high up. So all you can hear is silence, a serene silence with the birds and the wind in the trees. It makes you feel comfortable and content within that moment.'

The car turned the corner to find all the staff lined up outside, ready for his arrival. 'There were maybe ten members of staff and I thought I was really important. I thought, "Oh, they must have been told that I'm a great person or something." It was like going to a really fine hotel.'

The welcoming committee made him feel special. After two months of living in the darkness at home, this was the first time that he'd experienced a glimmer of hope that it could all finally change. Each staff member greeted him one by one and made him feel more special than he had in months. He was elated. 'I remember the house manager coming to the car to open the door saying, "Welcome to Skircoat Lodge. This is your new home."' He stops mid-sentence as he's talking to me. 'There's that word again: home.' He pauses, then carries on explaining the house manager's welcome speech: '"This is your new home. You're going to be fine here and we're gonna have a great time."' And just like that, he was ushered quickly through the front doors with his social worker to meet the cleaners and kitchen staff. He finally felt his light returning. 'I thought, "This is my new home."'

Well, yes, on a surface level this was his new 'home'. But not one that he was used to; in fact it wasn't a home that most of us are used to. Once he'd walked through that door the picture-perfect façade began to fade, quickly. He remembers the strong smell of bleach in his new home, as they made their way through to the office. A young boy came to show him around, and Chris says the boy's lifeless tone unnerved him: 'He was eleven years old – there should have been a bit of life, a bit of spring, but there was nothing there.' They made their way through the building and eventually came to the dorm rooms, with their curtain-less windows, beds covered in plastic, and all door handles removed. Upon Chris asking why this was the case, the boy simply replied, 'Oh, you'll find out,' and left it at that.

Within days the façade had completely dropped and the reality of what his home *really* was became clear. And it scared him. None of the boys wanted a conversation, no one wanted to talk at all, and his dreams of this place becoming his new home of love and security ebbed away. 'Say you watch *Oliver!* or *Annie* and everybody's jumping around and dancing. That's in the back of your mind. You think that's what it's gonna be like. Like that scene in *Annie* where they're all jumping on the beds at night-time. But there was total fear of even getting up. I remember one of the boys going "Sssh, you've gotta be quiet now. Gotta be quiet." And I'm thinking, why do I need to be quiet? "If you don't, if you're not quiet, they'll come in and they'll hit you."'

Chris realised it was a dangerous place. The badness in the world that his family had shielding him from was right in front of him, he was living in it. There wasn't much that he could do about it. And the lack of curtains and those plastic bed sheets? Years later, Chris realised that the first was to prevent the boys from hanging themselves, while the second was to stop the boys bleeding all over the mattress, having been raped. This was the place Chris now called home.

He was hit in the head by a staff member for incorrectly buttering toast; he was locked in a police cell overnight for smoking a cigarette; on day three he was shut in a cupboard for arguing with a staff member. 'I was kept there eight hours, and given some crackers and some water. There's nothing there and you can't spread your arms out.' He spreads his arms out to show me how narrow it was. 'You get really claustrophobic because there's a little light at the top and it looks like it used to be a stationery cupboard or something. But the door had been removed and an oak door was put in place. So even if you're quite tough and strong you weren't going to kick it down. I was dragged in there on the third day. On the fourth day, my social worker came to visit me and I told her everything that had happened in the last three days. I said I wanted to go back home to my mum. She called me a liar.'

He then goes on to tell me about a game the staff would play among themselves to earn points: if they hit you with a cricket bat with enough force to knock you down in one go, they'd earn ten points. If they hit you and *didn't* knock you down in one go, they'd *lose* ten points, 'I saw that happen to all these kids. Staff would walk past you and smack you round the face, then hit you in the legs with a cricket bat so that you'd go down.'

The dichotomy between the home he knew, and the reality he was faced with at his new home of Skircoat Lodge was stark.

'I missed the smell of my home, even though my mum was in a bad place, mentally – I missed knowing she was there. I missed the couch, and the carpets where I used to sit with Dad. I missed my dartboard. I missed my attic where we used to go. And I just wanted to be back there. Life was different, and it was taken from me overnight without any kind of explanation as to why. And I was put in this place where, to this day, I don't know what [it] was exactly. But it definitely wasn't a home.'

And that's the profound effect of growing up in a home where you feel safe and secure – when it's taken away from you before you're ready, it can have a profound life-changing impact on your life going forward. Your heart is tied to it and to its memories for ever, and the yearning for that never dissipates. It's frozen and suspended in time, and will be the blueprint and point of reference that carries you through life. When things seem pointless, dark or scary, those memories of youth before the darkness crept in – before real life entered into the equation – will seem like perfection. Even if it wasn't. Looking back can bring comfort in moments when it's so desperately needed.

It's Chris's happiness back then, now suspended in time for

ever, that he credits with giving him the strength and courage to survive Skircoat Lodge and eventually escape its angry and abusive claws. If he'd stayed longer there than the handful of months he endured, his memories of what a life full of joy could be, and the hope that he could have that again, would have been beaten out of him. Sexual violence would have ensured that any desire to build that life again would have shattered into small pieces – never to be seen whole again. If you can't remember what joy feels like, if you can't remember what being safe and secure feels like, the darkness can become so powerful that peace can seem lost for ever.

But Chris still had his memories, and the wherewithal to understand what was happening in Skircoat Lodge. He'd seen boys being taken off for the day for 'an adventure' with a key worker and either never returning or coming back changed in a way he couldn't quite comprehend. But he understood that whatever had happened wasn't right.

He remembers two boys going missing from his dorm: 'I never understood where they were. I thought they'd gone on an adventure and not asked me to go with them. But then I found out they'd been taken away and severely raped. [Later,] I was told I was going to be taken treasure hunting. And I knew what treasure hunting meant. I was gonna be taken out by a social worker, a key worker. He used to come and take boys out. I knew something wasn't right. Why was I going to be taken away all day by this man? And I ran away that day. I never went back to the home ever again.'

What Chris didn't know then but understands now is that he saved his own life that day. At twelve years old, with no adults to help him navigate the situation he was in, he took charge of his own destiny and left. Years later, in 1997, 'Operation Screen' was opened by police. Head of the home Malcolm Phillips and social worker Andrew Shalders were both jailed for a total of twenty-two years for the child abuse of boys and girls at the Lodge.

During the 1990s and into the twenty-first century, Skircoat was one of many children's homes which were revealed to be the locations of widespread abuse. Investigations were triggered across the UK, but also in other countries such as Ireland, Canada and Australia. Even today, historical instances of abuse in organisations and institutions where children *should* have been safe continue to be exposed. Report after report, inquiry after inquiry reveal the inability of those in positions of power to believe or notice children being abused under professional care.[1]

Britain's history of abuse and paedophilia scandals in its care homes from the 1960s to the early 1990s is dark, and as a result there are no longer any large residential homes. The nation which birthed the welfare state found itself in a situation where the most vulnerable in society were being sexually and physically abused on a horrific scale in institutions specifically created to keep them safe.

The issue of abuse in Britain's children's homes first came into the public view in 1989, just before Chris was driven to Skircoat. The case in question was the systemic abuse of children at Castle Hill School in Shropshire. In response to a number of complaints, police began to investigate the 'independent school' for young boys with behavioural and learning difficulties. Allegations of abuse were made by fifty-seven victims against Ralph Morris, principal and co-owner of the school. In 1991, Morris was sentenced to twelve years in prison on charges of physical, sexual and emotional abuse which went on for a number of years. It is thought that over that period of time, Morris and other staff abused hundreds of boys, with only fifty-seven feeling able to come forward. The sting in the tail for the children whose lives were impacted by the adults charged with looking after them was that Morris had completely fabricated his qualifications. No one had bothered to check, leaving him to do whatever he wanted to hundreds of kids who were unfortunate enough to pass through his doors, creating a trail of destruction.[2]

There is no single reason for the proliferation of paedophiles within the British care system after the 1960s, but there were specific decisions made which allowed the situation to flourish. Up until 1967, jobs in the care system were mostly taken on by women and most of the staff were live-in. That year, figures show that two-thirds of those employed in residential homes were single women, with a third of staff aged over fifty years old. With so many staff living on the premises at the time, the side-effect meant that they provided a safeguarding ring of steel around the children. Many of these women had worked in the industry their whole lives; some were war widows who had been left unmarried due to a shortage of men following the Second World War. In care homes they found not only employment, but also somewhere to live so they didn't have to be alone. But once they got older and retired, their jobs were largely taken by men because the roles had become full-time and were becoming mostly non-residential. Once these women left, it was almost as though the floodgates were opened. Paedophiles can spot a weakness in the system a mile away. This phenomenon was highlighted by Sir Andrew Kirkwood in his report into the abuse that took place in Leicestershire children's homes by the notorious sex offender Frank Beck, who was jailed in 1991.[3]

Hundreds of children are thought to have been abused under Beck's care, but it wasn't until 1989 that a complaint was taken seriously enough to warrant an investigation which led to Britain's largest investigation into institutionalised child abuse. Police took statements from nearly four hundred children who had been in his care during his twenty-year career as a social worker. Complaints had been made in the early 1980s, but had not been considered seriously.

In his report, Sir Andrew noted, 'the 1970s saw . . . a deliberate move away from the traditional arrangement whereby children's homes were in the hands of a husband-and-wife team as superintendent and matron, or officer in charge and deputy'. He cites this as one of the reasons for the rise in cases in children's homes across the country.

As a result, multiple investigations into these homes began, with police forces looking into allegations made by former residents in the 1970s and 1980s. However, even now, investigations are still ongoing: police admitted for the first time in 2020 that there was an 'epidemic' of institutional child sexual abuse in children's homes during that period, with Simon Bailey – the national lead for child protection and abuse investigations – saying, 'We do not understand the true scale of it . . . untold damage has been done to victims and survivors.'[4]

An all-party parliamentary group on Adult Survivors of Childhood Sexual Abuse talked of the impact the abuse had on survivors, now aged in their fifties, sixties and older, who have spent a lifetime with the knowledge that their horrific experiences were not believed. The ramifications of what many of them were subjected to in the place they were supposed to see as their home, the place they thought they'd be safe, would continue to affect many of them emotionally and psychologically for the rest of their lives.

In Chris's later years, he spent time searching for the boys he'd shared a dorm with. A search for their names on Facebook proved fruitless but he did eventually track down their relatives. What they told him, though, shocked him: most had taken their own lives by the age of twenty-one. 'There were six boys in that bedroom. Only two of us are still alive and one of them really, you know, suffered. I am very, very lucky to have survived such a horrible experience. But I'm just one of hundreds who were subjected to that kind of abuse in that children's home for over thirty years.'

Skircoat Lodge was eventually sold and bought by developers. That building was supposed to be a physical embodiment of the home the children had left behind. It was supposed to represent the safety and security they had perhaps not had the privilege to experience in their lives before. It was supposed to be the lifeboat they so desperately needed, the hug from a grown-up that would shield them from the bad stuff. Instead, the home and its adults *were* the bad stuff, and the home that was supposed to protect them became the place that destroyed them.

Somehow, throughout his stay at Skircoat, Chris managed to keep hold of his dad's chain: a physical reminder of the hero that he'd lost, and the life he once had. It was unfortunately stolen in his teens, but he describes it to me as similar to the Star of David. Not because his family was from a Jewish background, but because his dad *was* 'a star'. Holding onto it during moments of fear made Chris feel safe, so he carried it with him through most of his childhood. His father's chain and the memories of his home life were Chris's life raft, enabling him to continue treading water to stay alive even when the domino effect of his father's passing continued. Upon leaving the children's home behind, he was rendered homeless at just twelve years old.

I'm not sure if I would have had the wherewithal to survive the next few years like Chris did. He entered his teens homeless and living on the streets, with only himself to rely on. At this stage of his story, I can't help but compare it with what I was doing in the same year, during what was a pivotal stage in my life: I'd discovered the joy of sneaking into my mum's room and putting on a hint of red lipstick. It was the height of the school disco era and under-eighteens house parties. It was the year I realised I'd started my period, right at the end of my athletics class, and dealt with it so calmly it freaked my mum out a bit. All in all, it was a busy year. But I didn't just have myself to rely on. At home, I had two grown-ups who were still trying their hardest to envelop me in their arms and keep me safe from seeing and understanding the bad stuff in the world. My home provided solace in a way I probably didn't fully comprehend until I reached adulthood. I had a bedroom covered in posters of music artists – with the likes of Toni Braxton, Mariah Carey and Whitney Houston blaring out of my radio. My favourite teddy bears chucked on my bed ready to be cuddled as I slept at night. Despite the usual ups and downs of teenage-dom I was content, but most importantly – I was safe.

I believe that steadies you in a way that it's probably difficult to fully comprehend. Knowing that home is your safe and secure place allows you to dabble in the dalliances of youth, allows you to push the boundaries a bit more because you know at the end of the day your home will always be there for you. It's the place that will welcome you back with all the trappings of familiarity, as long as you don't push those dalliances too far. Having that grounding in your formative years accounts for so much of who we become later on in life. That love that surrounds you like a ring of steel within those four walls allows you to be the child you're supposed to be. Despite Chris's ring of steel being forcibly broken apart aged eleven, he was old enough to know what having it felt like. He was also mature enough to understand what he'd lost when it was gone, and according to him, despite the brevity of his fulfilling home life, it was enough to sustain him through to adulthood, and helped him survive on the streets, hanging out with other boys his age who'd also found themselves homeless. 'That's what made me different to a lot of these boys. A lot of these boys were born into a world of evil, but I wasn't. I was born into a world of love.' He'd been given so much love in that home in those short few years that it didn't run out when he needed those memories to carry him through.

After leaving Skircoat Lodge at twelve, Chris spent the following four years making his way through Halifax's streets with other boys who were also trying to survive. His world revolved around shoplifting food to eat, finding things to sell, fitting through small windows to steal stuff from houses, and sleeping on random sofas in strangers' houses or drug dens. When times were bad, the only safe places were sleeping *behind* bins or sleeping *in* bins. He says that throughout that time he kept holding onto his dad's chain, not only to remind him of his hero, but to also make sure he kept those memories alive so that he wouldn't forget that life used to be more than what he was currently being dealt.

The thing about growing up in a home that makes you feel safe and secure is that there can be an understandable need to recreate that in life later on. It's like you can cherry-pick the pieces you liked and get rid of the bits you don't, forming your own new jigsaw puzzle of the bits you want to salvage for your own life and your own children. And what's apparent about Chris's story is his need to do the same, that drive and desire to recover what was so cruelly taken away, so he could get himself back onto an even keel.

One story he tells me about a Christmas he spent on the streets is demonstrative of that. 'I was walking the streets on Christmas Day, just looking at people's windows and seeing their Christmas tree and families, and I got upset and emotional about it. But I told myself, "You're gonna have it yourself one day, don't worry, your time will come." So I just kept looking – not in a scary way where people are going to end up calling the police – but just walking past and seeing it and observing it and thinking, "I want that back so much."' He then took himself back to his bedsit and had his Christmas Day Pot Noodle on his own. But his determination to get back the home that was stolen from him never waned.

For Chris, the home that he yearned for was not just about four walls and parents – it was so much more than that. 'What is love as a child? It's not just parents giving you a hug and telling you they love you. It's that security, it's warmth. Visualising my old house in Boomtown in Halifax where I grew up with my dad is a safe place I take myself to sometimes. To have been on the couch and looking out the window to Square Park and seeing it was snowing – even now, just talking about it like that is a safe place. I can visualise it so well, everything about that moment: sat on the couch with my dad and my sister, my mum.' He takes a moment to find the right words. 'My safe place for me is the epitome of a home in that moment of time. That kind of security of having everything you could possibly need as a child is what home is, those foundations of "nothing can go wrong". Because you're safe in that moment. And that, for me, is what home was and still is.'

It's something that he searched and searched for as the years passed, and at sixteen years old he joined the Army – not to serve, but to find somewhere where he could feel safe again, somewhere he could sleep soundly and where he didn't have to search for food. 'I was surrounded by boys who didn't want anything from me: I didn't have to shoplift or break into a house or give them everything. They were just people who were genuinely concerned about me. All the boys had been through similar things to me and got through it. And so they became mentors in my life. It was a different way of living, where I realised, 'Oh, there is a light at the end of the tunnel, there is a pathway through what I've been through. That it's possible to break free and get your life back up and running again.'

At that same age, in that same year, I was thinking about

A-level choices, writing letters to get work experience and working out what I wanted to do at university. It was the same year my mum was diagnosed with bowel cancer, but even that wasn't enough to shatter the foundations of love, safety, and security that my parents had created in our home. It caused a tremor, of course, but it wasn't a big enough earthquake to bring the whole thing crashing down. Even with the diagnosis they were still trying their hardest to hug me tightly and protect me and my siblings from the bad stuff in the world. Even as a family living through cancer, that home protected us from all the other things that they thought we didn't have the maturity to handle. But Chris didn't have a choice. While I was mulling over degree options, his brief stint in the Army started the process of rebuilding his life, and giving him the emotional building blocks to start working towards his ultimate goal: a place he could call home again.

His face lights up when he describes, essentially, what rediscovering hope looks like. 'Back then, I'm getting on in life and becoming a young man, and I've gotta start thinking about the future. I'd never thought about the future before – it didn't exist, it was always a dream. But I became absolutely fearless and excited about everything I could achieve, everything I could do. I'd been in that moment of being homeless, so everything else was really exciting. Like what, you mean, I could get a job and buy a house?! Wow, this is amazing.' For the first time in a long time, even though it was for a short period, Chris began to feel at home.

For the first time since he was eleven years old, an adult had given him some semblance of security. '[The Army] became a home for a short period of time because it gave me some safety and security. The bed was safe at night-time, and there were curtains in my bedroom. There were all the people who cared for me and looked out for me.'

The advantage of growing up with the basics of a home – love, safety and security – means that we get the freedom to figure out who we want to be, and what shape our stamp on the world is going to look like. If we are forced into survival mode, as Chris was, you don't always have the emotional strength to plan your life, to plan your next steps. To just figure the world out. How can you, when every day you wake up it's a battle to get through the next twenty-four hours alive, and without getting locked up? When our minds are not just focused on surviving, it gives us the freedom to explore, and to understand who we are and our place in the world.

For Chris, a bed and six months of basic Army training at Penicuik in Edinburgh finally gave him that luxury. 'There's been these moments in my life where there's elation. It's a feeling of being comfortable and content and having that moment where the world is a beautiful place. And you start to like yourself again and think, you know what, the world isn't a bad place, and you're not a bad person.'

It is remarkable for Chris to reach adulthood knowing that a large chunk of his teens had been spent with people telling him he was bad. The impact and ramifications of that cannot be underestimated – routinely being told you're bad by those who should know better would no doubt be internalised by somebody so young. He'd been failed by the grown-ups who were meant to look after him, and instead it was the grown-ups who consistently made him feel less-than. It was the decisions repeatedly made by grown-ups that caused Chris' life to fall apart at the seams the moment his dad became ill. Those decisions wrenched him away from the one place he felt safe, secure, and loved, thrusting him onto a path that he neither asked for nor wanted.

He continues: 'You've got to find yourself again, and find things [that are] good about you again. I found I could smile, I wasn't anxious, and found that I was polite: I was becoming my dad again. It was a really good space to grow.' The Army pieced Chris together bit by bit until the strength that had been slowly but surely drained out of him year after year started to return.

He says that his beliefs fundamentally didn't align with the mission of the Army, the two didn't fit. But he will always be thankful for what it gave him – what he needed, finally. It was, though, to be a temporary home. He wanted and yearned for more, and so after six months of growing to love himself again, and through the encouragement of older recruits, he felt strong enough to seek out the family that he'd lost, and maybe, just maybe, he could find home again.

The memories of the home that was so cruelly taken from him was not where he immediately gravitated back to. Instead, it was his grandma's house. What he hadn't known at the time was that she had searched for him for years prior, but to no avail. But stepping into that house took him back in time: 'Grandma smells the same to this day: of roses and flowers.' He says he just walked in, and it smelt like home.

Ah, the smell of home. One of the most individual and difficult-to-replicate sensations there is. If you close your eyes and think of the home you grew up in, or one of the places you closely connect to the idea of home ... what do you smell? Interestingly, for me it's not the home I grew up in but my paternal grandma's home too. I hadn't really thought about it much before, even during the course of speaking to Chris. The sensation and realisation came weeks afterwards – it suddenly hit me during a visit to the home of a friend's grandma who's also originally from the Caribbean, but settled in Leicester.

'Grandma Vanessa' stepped out of her front porch to hug me and then motioned me inside. I was talking and laughing with her and some friends as I stepped in, stopped briefly – and then it hit me. As I stepped into the main part of the house, the smell just crept up my nose and seemed to take over my body. It smelt like home. It smelt *exactly* like my grandma's home (she passed back in 2015). And it's going to sound so bizarre, but the smell was Mr Sheen, mixed with just-cooked Caribbean food – in this case, a large batch of fried dumplings for her guests. But in all honesty, it was the layers and layers of Mr Sheen being plastered all over the plethora of framed pictures that adorned the walls, the shelves, the tables, the floor, and any other flat surface you could find in the living room. Every single one had clearly been painstakingly wiped with Mr Sheen ahead of our visit; and not just that, but every inch of the leather sofas in the living room. It was exactly like being at my grandma's, with Vanessa's many grandchildren proudly on display in school photos and university graduation photos, and her children's pictures spanning the various decades of their lives. It was like I'd been transported back twenty years and was stood in my own grandma's living room.

I walked through the kitchen, and everything was as it

could have been at my grandma's house too. I instinctively opened drawers to grab cutlery and plates, and it was like having muscle memory, but in a place I'd never set foot in before. Everything was where it would have been had I been stood in my grandma's kitchen. And it hit me hard. I hadn't expected it, and wasn't prepared for it. Unbeknownst to anyone in the room, it took me a while to sit down on the sofa – I kept milling around finding things to do and stuff to look at. I just found it hard. It was a familiar smell in an unfamiliar house, and it unnerved me a bit. My grandma and I were close, and having spent so much of my childhood in her house, being at Vanessa's just reminded me of everything I hadn't had in so long. And much like being at my grandma's, I knew that sitting on the sofa would bring me closer to the smell and I just didn't have the strength to do it in those first few minutes of being in Vanessa's house.

But when you've got a plate full of fried chicken, dumplings, curry goat, rice and peas, coleslaw and whatever else I glutinously served myself from the table, you can't stand to eat. It's a physical mission that's genuinely just not worth it. So I finally sat down and the sensation was overwhelming, if I'm honest. I'm a bit emotional writing this all down now. The smells suddenly all meshed into one, and as I reached down to the arm of the leather sofa chair and ran my fingers over it, that familiar silky feeling of Mr Sheen'd leather left its mark on my fingertips. And it made me smile.

Even though there was so much of this room that reminded me of home, it *wasn't* home, and once the initial shock had subsided, I noticed the differences and my emotions lessened.

Because of this, when Chris talks about his grandma's

house I completely get it. For him, her house had been frozen in time. Although he remembered the smell, he was a young innocent child the last time he saw it ... and when he returned, he was still technically a child, but had been thrown a hand that had seen him mature beyond his years. Physically too, he had changed. He was no longer a small eleven-year-old boy – he was bigger and broader, and took up more space.

'Going back, it didn't feel as empty as it used to be, you know. I had grown. It still felt safe and secure, but I was different, you know? I was different and I didn't belong there any more. I'd grown out of it.'

You remember things as being so much bigger when you're a child, don't you? The home you grew up in can seem huge, but if you leave and return as an adult you see it with such different eyes. Would you still fit into those memories that you had held dear, and would it then have the same pull emotionally? As much as Chris had wanted his return to his grandma's to be that missing piece of the puzzle that he had been yearning for for so many years, he couldn't have possibly accounted for just how much he'd changed physically and emotionally. So he left, searching for the place that would fill his heart and make him feel whole again.

He found lots of temporary 'homes' in his search in the following years, but nothing that gave him the sensation that he was looking for: being at home with his dad. It was a big ask, but I get it. As someone who lost a parent way before they should have left, you do almost find yourself on a constant search to recreate what you had. But it was a search that Chris was determined to complete.

The search took him to his first flat, aged eighteen, in Halifax. He smiles when he recalls his time there: 'I didn't have a clue how to keep it, and didn't know what bills were. I remember sitting on the toilet and realising there was no toilet roll: I'd taken it for granted that somebody else would put it there. In the Army the cleaners had replaced it, at home Mum replaced it, at Grandma's she'd replace it, and on the streets you didn't really care.'

There are lots of things that are broken with the care system in the UK. Chris's example is one of many. It's a system no government seems to be able to get right. And once kids have left the system at eighteen (or sixteen, if they choose), adapting to 'real life' can be a relentlessly uphill and painful transition. Few parents would happily let their child out into the world at eighteen with very little support, but at that age the local authority is no longer considered to be their 'corporate parent'. So if they want to build a home they can finally call their own, they had to learn to adapt in order to survive.

For Chris it was a challenge he thrived on: 'I took to it like a duck to water.' His dad's traits are clearly very much a part of him all these years later. 'I absolutely loved being in control of it. I found it incredibly difficult at first. I'd gone from being in care to being homeless and not having huge responsibilities like paying electric, water, rent and things like that. I had to learn how to do it all.' A third of care leavers become homeless in the first two years immediately after they leave care,[5] and 25 per cent of people who are homeless have spent some point in their life in care. The odds were stacked against Chris, 'but I was intrigued, I was like a sponge', always learning.

Chris's journey into adulthood, and the beginnings of him learning to create a home of his own, is beautiful to listen to. Those first few years tentatively taking steps towards the life he'd been craving clearly mean a lot to him. He learnt to cook, and even now prides himself on his cookery skills. Unsurprisingly, he learnt to get joy from the simplest of meals because he was making the decisions in his own home, finally in charge of himself, no matter how little money he had to create something. 'I remember being in my own flat on a Saturday night when everybody else was out drinking and doing whatever they're doing, I'd make two crisp sandwiches, drink a pint of milk and watch cheap videos I'd got for two pounds.' The joy he got from those moments is infectious when you hear him speak.

He takes great pride in the construction of his crisp sandwich, a meal which more than twenty years later he still reaches for in moments when he craves solace and comfort. He talks me through it: 'Please don't judge me when I say this: I used to get turkey ham, white bread, cheese and onion crisps and mayo. I'm sorry, a classic is a classic!' I laugh, because adding crisps to my sandwich is a weekly occurrence for me, despite the odd looks I get when I'm sat in the office carefully opening my sandwich to painstakingly add each individual crisp, then biting into perfection. Adding crisps elevates *any* sandwich, and both Chris and I will take on anyone who dares to argue otherwise.

It gets me thinking about the cheaper meals that my parents grew up with that we had regularly as kids, that I still yearn for when I'm having a wobble emotionally and just need something that reminds me of that time in my life when mum was still at home. And for me that's corned beef and rice – also known as bully beef and rice. Simply a can of corned beef cooked up with onions, peppers, sweetcorn and Scotch bonnet chillies, served on a bed of white rice. When the corned beef hits the pan and starts sizzling, the smell that fills my kitchen just takes me back. The very essence of Caribbean food is creating something out of virtually nothing, and wasting nothing, but corned beef and rice is something special for me.

Perhaps because he's older and in a completely different situation in his life, Chris can talk with an incredible amount of fondness for a time in his life that clearly wasn't ever easy for someone so young. But, for him, it was the start of living his life on his own terms: the tough times where brown sauce was the only ingredient in his sandwiches, and his ability to turn a Pot Noodle into a two-course meal (you eat the noodles, then use the bottom bit for soup served with bread) built on the survival skills he'd clearly learnt as a young teen on the streets.

But it's when he starts talking about the pivotal moment in his life which changed everything that his whole demeanour shifts. The night he met the woman who is now his wife. It sounds like something from a movie, but she walked into a bar in London he was working in aged thirty-one and, he says, 'I fell love instantly.' He had, up until that point pulled away from any situation where his heart would be in the hands of another: 'I'd only ever known dysfunction. I didn't want to hurt anybody.' Despite desperately searching for a home that would replicate what he'd lost, he'd been actively pushing it away in case it all fell apart again. Trauma can find ways to grip onto you with all its might, no matter how much you *need* it to leave so that you can truly start afresh. But that doesn't happen until you're ready.

It was on their first date, when she intimated that what had happened to him before was not going to define their future, that the switch happened, both in Chris's mind and heart: 'What that gave me in that moment was a sense of, "Oh my God, somebody loves me for me. Somebody wants to be with me. Somebody believes in me."' He pauses. 'That's what's so powerful as a human being. For somebody to say, "It's all right, you're not alone."'

From the moment social workers walked Chris out of his home at eleven years old, that is what he'd been longing for. Twenty years later, on a first date in London, his heart finally allowed him to let go. And the start of *finally* building a home, his home, began.

Within a year they were married and had their first child, two huge deals for anyone who finally finds love. Listening to Chris describe this just makes me want to hug him so tightly, and when he talks about the odds that were against him ever reaching this moment, I know he's right. But it feels as though it was the dogged determination to get the joy that a family and a home could bring back into his life that kept him going. Throughout *all* of it, throughout everything that had happened to him, that was the thing that steadfastly remained in his heart and his head. He never gave up hope that he would get it again.

And telling me this part of his story is the part that chokes him up: getting back the one thing he'd been wanting since it was ripped from him as a young teenager – a home.

'I'm not religious, but I think there must be something there, someone guiding me to this moment. Because how does somebody like me fall into these situations and come out smelling of roses, and be guided to this moment in time, in history, where I meet this amazing woman?'

In that first year of meeting, not only did they hit all the milestones of being in a relationship – marriage and a baby – they also bought a house. After all the nightmares that Chris had managed to push through, the darkness that threatened to engulf him, came the light. As he starts to tell me his voice breaks; all these years later the magnitude of that moment – putting his *own* key into his *own* door of his *own* home that will house his *own* family – is still as strong. 'How does that happen without somebody wishing it for you and guiding you towards it, like more of a spiritual thing?'

So many people dream of having their own home someday, but for Chris it's different. It means more than just four walls to lay his head, more than just an investment for the future. It means new beginnings, a chance to try again. A chance to finish what his dad started. 'I never wanted to be a footballer, I never wanted to be rich, and I never wanted to be famous. I just wanted a key to my "home-home" that nobody could take off me. To have a family that I can have control of and bring up and support. It's the best thing I've ever had in my life.'

Whether you're religious or spiritual or none of the above, there's a part of the grief process that hopes the individual hasn't gone for ever. That they're perhaps somewhere still helping to guide us in some way or another. I often think that my mum sends special people into my life for a reason, and throughout difficulties with both my pregnancies I begged her to make sure the kids were okay. You like to think that even if they're not physically here, there's still a presence of sorts touching your shoulder or gripping your arm so that you're never truly alone. Especially in your darkest moments. You hope that they are somewhere in a room, perhaps leaning against a wall looking proudly on, as you celebrate a milestone. I believe my mum is still with me in both the brightest and darkest moments in my life. Chris believes his dad's presence has somehow guided him to where he is now. When so many adults failed him when he needed them most, it appears as though it is the memory of a man, who was taken from his life all those years ago, who is the *one* adult who stayed with him to make sure he was okay.

'Every day in my life is magical. It's not always easy – when you have a house and get married, and you have a family it's incredibly complicated. But for me it's like, wow, thank you. Thank you. Whoever guided me to this, thank you.'

Chapter 3

An Immigrant by Choice

Whether you're fleeing war, or if you've made the choice to move to a new home in a different country, there will always be an adjustment period. My parents juggled quite a few when they arrived as teenagers – the blatant and covert racism, adapting to the weather, familiarising themselves with the food, getting used to the customs, the list was exhaustive and endless. Each person that arrives in Britain from elsewhere will have a story that involves trying to adapt to being here. Wanting to be part of Britain does not and should not mean that you want to lose your cultural heritage. It can be a difficult balance to strike between full assimilation into British tradition and retaining your own culture. A common example is from one of my closest friends, Saima – her mum is from Pakistan, and every year they observe Ramadan. But every December they also celebrate Christmas. One does not cancel out the other, there is space for both.

So, me growing up in a Jamaican home in a corner of London doesn't mean that my parents were rejecting life in the UK – they were preserving their traditions and way of life, while also taking on the traditions of the country which they had been moved to by their parents. My dad gravitated towards the Jamaican guys at the Ford Dagenham plant where he worked, because strength in numbers meant there was slightly less stress racism-wise. But also, they could share stories of home with each other with first-hand knowledge. And when you're thousands of miles from that home, that can bring solace to someone who's going through bouts of homesickness. You can both miss somewhere and enjoy where you are at the same time. Again, the two situations are not mutually exclusive.

It's why when immigrants move, they tend to base themselves in areas where they are already well represented. For instance, the Swedish School in London. The city's Swedish community is among the highest concentration of Swedes outside of their home country – in fact, London is known for having the largest Swedish population outside Sweden. It would, therefore, make sense that newer Swedes arriving in the UK would gravitate towards the capital city. There is a level of comfortableness that comes with being able to share traditions like Kråftskiva (Sweden's crayfish party), for example. As a result of the high concentration of Swedes, the UK's only Swedish school is located in the capital. Its history goes back more than a century. A slice of Swedish tradition and home life squeezed into a corner of London.

It's not dissimilar to Brits who emigrate elsewhere in the world and become immigrants themselves. Take Spain for example, home to one of the largest British-born populations outside of the UK in the world. You'll find large concentrations of British people in places like Andalusia and the Costa Del Sol. There's a certain amount of comfort, for some, being among those with whom they have a shared knowledge of life back home, and, of course, language. Many of them never have to learn Spanish, despite decades of living there, because they can get by quite easily without it – mostly due to living in pockets of Britain, within Spain.

The same applies with my family. There are pockets of Caribbean and African communities right across the UK for that very reason. London has the highest concentration of Jamaicans, followed by the West Midlands, and then the South-West.

The story of why these areas have high concentrations can be traced back to when *Empire Windrush* docked at Tilbury in Essex, the primary port for London. This made the capital the most popular destination for the 802 passengers on board from the Caribbean[1] who were looking for work and lodgings, but a few headed to places like Liverpool, Manchester, Birmingham – poorer areas with enough work to go round. In areas such as Bristol they were able to find poor housing in places like St Paul's and Easton because the area and its buildings had been so badly damaged during the war, and landlords were more likely to rent to them.

In the 1950s, Brixton became the hub for the Caribbean community who moved to the UK, with Jamaicans in particular choosing the area to become their home. Its markets became a Mecca for fruits, vegetables, and produce that many struggled to find elsewhere. The constant hum of reggae and roots playing from morning until night became the soundtrack to the Jamaican immigrant experience: its tapestry of sounds, smells, and sights so different from what had come before. The impact was palpable, so much so that in 1956 when Mrs Edna

Marlene, the wife of Jamaica's then-Chief Minister, visited the area she said she 'was surprised to see them [West Indians] buying sweet potato and tinned ackee ... it was like a little bit of home'. Confirmation, if ever, that the work that had been put in to create their own little corner of home in a country which had shunned and belittled them, had been successful.[2]

My maternal grandparents moved to London because they knew people living there who had already made the move, so it made it easier to find rooms to rent in an environment that was otherwise vehemently against renting to immigrants. Social housing wasn't an option for those British subjects; they were deemed not British enough to benefit from it. Friends who had arrived before my grandparents who then went on to buy properties would rent rooms to new arrivals, until those newcomers had saved enough to buy their own homes and pass the kindness on to the next influx of new arrivals. Eventually though, the harsh racism eased slightly, meaning more rental options became available.

By the time my parents met there was no reason to move away, because the homes in the area were still affordable back then, and so they stayed. As did their friends and extended family. My generation, though, is different: high property prices mean many of my friends and family who were born and raised in south-east London have been forced to settle elsewhere. The areas that were once poor and working class in London have become richer and therefore unaffordable to those who had called it home for most of their lives.

The latest census data (2021) shows that 'ethnic segregation' in England and Wales is on the decrease, as more people now live alongside neighbours from different backgrounds.

There are so many reasons why that could be happening, and finances are part of that, but also, perhaps, generationally people are not so 'scared' of sharing environments with those they don't resemble, with fewer marches dedicated to 'getting the foreigners out'. In fact, the census showed that neighbourhood diversity had more than doubled between 2001 and 2021. Places like Boston in Lincolnshire have seen a tenfold increase in diversity (though from a low base).[3]

As to whether the pockets will develop again, only time will tell what communities will look like with the generations to come. But for now, when you're in areas or environments where diversity is sparse, sometimes the 'Nod' is all to need to feel at home. It's an almost indecipherable lowering of the head, in acknowledgement of another Black person on the street when your paths cross. It doesn't matter where you are in the world, it's the universal sign of solidarity, and one which I use regularly. It's a mark of respect, in acknowledgement of being the 'only ones'.

Due to my work, I can end up in areas with low levels of diversity quite often, and as soon as I walk past another Black person I give them the Nod, and they do the same in return. It's almost like saying, 'I got you,' without ever having to utter a word. It can feel like an invisible cloak of protection when the colour of your skin can make you feel vulnerable in that moment.

When I lived in Norwich in my late twenties I was very much the only Black in the village. Only Norwich isn't a village, it's a city. As beautiful as it was, and as much I made friends there, I missed living in a more diverse area, which just made me even more homesick. I would return to London on the weekend with probably more frequency than I should have, to be honest.

But one afternoon I was wandering around the city's shops on my lunchbreak, when I suddenly saw a gorgeous Black woman walking towards me and smiling. We both did the Nod and I carried on, but she then doubled back and tapped me on the shoulder. 'Sorry, but where did you get your hair done? I've struggled so much to find somewhere decent to get my hair done,' she laughed. I apologised and explained that I return to London to get my hair done for that very reason. We then became firm friends.

A simple respectful nod gave me my first Black friend in East Anglia. I wouldn't necessarily say the action immediately made me feel like I'd found a home, because although Neide and I were similar ages we were at very different stages in our lives – she had two children, whereas I was footloose and fancy-free. But we were connected by shared experiences, especially those which related to being one one of very few Black women in the area. We were very used to being mistaken for other Black women who local people had met in their daily lives. Having that level of familiarity in your life can feel visceral. Not that other friends I met didn't mean the world to me, it was just, different.

I was reminded of an immigrant's initial need to seek out familiarity when they set up a new home, when I spoke to Nchedochukwu Moses Ikechukwu about his experience of making two big international moves within the space of three years in his thirties. The first of which, just before Covid, was his first-ever experience of anywhere other than the country of his birth.

Though it wasn't his first experience of living outside of the Delta State region of Nigeria where he was born. It's an oil and agricultural area in the south of the country. As Moses describes it, it's a cultural mix of tribes including Igbo, Itsekiri, Hausa, Urhobo, and a region which shares eleven different languages. It's one of the most developed states in Nigeria.

It's this environment in which Moses (as he prefers to be called) grew up. He was one of seven children, but doesn't describe his home as chaotic at all – it appears to have been more regimented: the strictness of a Nigerian household very much a feature of his childhood (I hear you, Moses).

'Yes, it was busy, but everyone knew their roles. You knew your time to mess around and your time to do your duties. Nobody had to tell anybody what to do, because you knew what you were supposed to do, and if you didn't do it you'd get smacked.' We both laugh at this point; there's a lot of discipline crossover between West African and Caribbean parenting in the '90s.

At thirteen years old, he was sent to Lagos to live with his uncle and go to secondary school. He says he remembers being enthralled by the tall buildings in the city, which were very different to the two- or three-level buildings he was used to in Delta State.

When he returned to Lagos for university, he was older and more able to understand the city from an adult's point of view: it made him miss the community feeling he'd left behind in Delta State, with the older generation having time to sit and retell stories to the younger generation as they all sat around socialising in the evening. He missed his friends. As excited as he was to be in a big city, it didn't quite seem like home for him: Moses and the big city had very different vibes. 'In Lagos,' he says, 'everybody was on the move. They didn't want to retell stories; everybody wanted to make a living. It was all work, work, work, with little time for idle chit-chat.'

It was never his plan, though, to leave Nigeria after university. A random direct message on Instagram triggered a series of events that would eventually see him catapulted across the sea for work, which would lead him to meeting his future wife, which then led to him moving to London where the couple are now settling. Suddenly he found himself alone, in completely unfamiliar environments, desperately trying to find the familiar.

As a result of his love for fitness and health he became qualified to teach fitness and dance professionally, and the videos he posted of these classes began to gain momentum online. Out of the blue, a large hotel resort contacted him via DM saying they were looking for a new teacher and was he interested? His first thought was, 'definitely a scam', especially when the offer of five times his current salary came up via a Zoom call. (I'm not being funny, but that would have been my first thought too.) A lawyer friend investigated, and it turns out it was all real. The initial contact was in December, by January his visa was sorted, and by February he was on his first ever flight out of Nigeria.

Moses takes one look at my shocked face and laughs. 'I know. Crazy, right?!' He landed in Dubai and his eyes were open to a whole new world. As somebody who had never lived or experienced being among anybody *other* than Nigerians his entire life, for the first time ever he wasn't the majority, he was the minority.

'It stressed me,' he explains. 'It was like being in one room for twenty to thirty years, and one day they just open the door and say, "Come out, there are other rooms in this house."' Suddenly everything was different for him, from the environment to the people. He says it felt like everything changed in a split-second. It was a feeling he hadn't expected and he had to learn to manage that and deal with it. 'It took me three months to think, okay, I'm here,' he laughs.

Any homesickness he felt was made worse when, not long after he arrived, the coronavirus pandemic began to spread internationally, and Dubai went into lockdown. He'd had this huge life-changing event that he was still trying to get his head round, but then, 'I was stuck in one place for eight months.' Everything, including the hotel where he was now employed, was closed. What helped though was there were three other hotel workers in the building: one from the local area and two from Ukraine. Together, they would sneak down the road to the beach so that they could get some sunlight, but the beach security would always send them back. It wasn't the life he had envisaged for himself when he made the decision to create a new home somewhere else. But he did the best that he could.

Food was a barrier that he expected to get over quite quickly. 'Nigerians are everywhere,' he begins to explain, 'so the first thing you have to do is work out where all the Nigerians are, where they eat their food, and who prepares the food.' As I understand it from his explanation, if you find a group of Nigerians in an area, one person will be in charge of cooking Nigerian food while the others in the group will facilitate buying the ingredients. Therefore everyone can have a taste of home. Covid, though, thwarted that usually reliable plan of action.

For Moses, it meant it took him a year to find somewhere to buy food from home. In that time, he lived on a diet of biryanis, which, although he enjoyed, didn't fill the emotional pull and the overwhelming feeling of yearning for flavours from home.

That is something that I can completely relate to – that inexplicable urge to just have a taste from home. It's not a wave that passes over you daily, but when it does hit that can be *all* you think about that day: it feels like a small hole in the pit of your stomach, that can only be filled by a taste or smell of home.

Early on in my career I was working on the south coast in Southampton for a few months. I was renting a room in possibly one of the most random houses in the city, near the port. The owner was a porn film director (told you it was random), and would spend large chunks of his time working away from home, so I basically had the place to myself with a single bed in his spare room. He did very kindly offer his bedroom as the one to rent since he was never around, but I took one look at the giant waterbed in his double room and politely declined. I'd watched enough *Law & Order* episodes at that point in my life to know about the levels of bodily fluids which can stick around on inanimate objects.

As a result of renting a room, his kitchen with all his stuff in it was available for me to use. It was a great kitchen (he had great taste, he clearly enjoyed 'entertaining'), but his cupboards had none of the seasonings that I was used to for cooking. It meant that I couldn't prepare any of the meals that I'd have at home with Mum and Dad. And London was two hours away. Trips to the local supermarket quickly highlighted the fact that I was not going to be able to get hold of things like all-purpose seasoning, pimento seeds or Scotch bonnet.

I was twenty and living away from home for the first time, so the homesickness was really hard at times. I had to keep resisting the urge to just jump in the car and drive home for dinner. By this point, my mum had been having treatment for four years (she died the following year) so our little family unit had become closer in the midst of trying to have some semblance of normality while juggling regular life with a parent who was going through so much pain. That's why it was my first time living away from home, as I'd made the decision not to go away for university since I couldn't leave the family for such a long period of time.

This possibly explains why I didn't have the foresight to actually *bring* the spices I needed with me, which, of course, would have made my life far easier. Much like Moses, I figured if I found the Black people, I'd find at least one Caribbean take-away. And even if the meal from there was rubbish, I genuinely didn't care if it just *smelt* like home and tasted awful, and I could also gather intel about the local Caribbean food shops.

But I was the only Black journalist in the newsroom where I was working, which meant that there wasn't anyone to get advice from. There was, however, a young journalist called Saima who worked there. She was also from London, and of Pakistani origin. As soon as I mentioned my dilemma, she understood my need straight away. She got out a map and pinpointed where in the city she had finally found halal meat. She figured if there was a big enough Muslim population in that area to warrant a halal butchers, other ethnic minorities must be nearby. These are the sort of Jessica Fletcher-esque clues that only ethnic minorities will appreciate.

Those of a certain age will wonder why I didn't just type

'local Caribbean takeaways' into Google. Well, clever clogs, that little internet perk didn't exist yet. As a result I jumped in my car with my circled map and headed out on the open road. I found the halal butchers and just kept driving.

Yep, I just kept driving around until I found what I was looking for: a group of Black people. I pulled over to ask for advice and, lo and behold, they pointed me in the direction of the nearest Caribbean takeaway. I could have cried. It was a big moment for me.

Once there, I ordered my usual: oxtail and rice, my go-to in new Caribbean takeaways. You have to leave the oxtail to cook down long enough for it to just fall off the bone. But it also has to be the perfect combination of seasonings, and not too salty or spicy, with the correct ratio of meat to butterbeans. If they mess that up, then for me it's an indication that they don't know what they're doing, and I never go back.

My Southampton oxtail experience wasn't quite perfection in terms of quality, but to be honest it didn't even matter at that point. As soon as I walked through the doors of the takeaway, that familiar smell of a Jamaican kitchen wafted up my nose, the sound of the lady on the till cussing out the chef behind her filled my ears, and dancehall was belting out from the radio on the counter. It was exactly what I needed at that moment in time. Within a second, I felt euphoric. I'd found a little slice of home, and that aching hole in the pit of my stomach filled ever so slightly. With a full belly in more ways than one, I slept well that night.

As a result, I can completely understand Moses' plan, and for him, it worked. He found someone who was able to tell him where the Nigerian community congregated in

Dubai – and it was his keen sense of smell for Nigerian food that sealed the deal and led him to discover the information he was after.

It happened one day at work (post-lockdown). Moses walked into the canteen and was hit by a familiar smell, 'and I just thought, no, no, it can't be. It's not possible.' Moses is actually killing himself laughing at this point of retelling the story. 'I turned round, then turned back and walked straight up to the colleague holding the dish from which the familiar smell was emanating from and said, "Bro, where did you get this stuff?"' The man in question was the only other Nigerian staff member at this huge hotel, and the meal he was eating is a very well-known dish called Egusi soup – a West African staple. It's a traditional dish of blended melon seeds, a pepper mix, veg and meat which is often served with pounded yam. The frequency with which it is served in Nigerian homes means that the smell is hugely identifiable.

Moses' obvious joy at finally finding a slice of home saw the man invite Moses to share the meal with him, a gesture that's beautiful in so many ways. The staff member had been working at the hotel for a lot longer than Moses and had therefore been in the country longer than him too, so his knee-jerk reaction of offering to share his meal feels like the actions of someone who had a very clear recollection of what it felt like to miss home in those first few months of leaving it. Moses hadn't had any food from home for a whole year, so that moment in time sticks firmly in his head. He was so thankful, 'I just thought, oh my God, *this* is food.' With the first half of Moses' mission complete, he got the location details of where he could find the ingredients he so desperately wanted to get his hands on, 'and from that day on I started going there every day. I never ate food from the hotel again.'

When he first found the area in question, he got the same euphoric experience I did that day in Southampton. 'I saw the shops and I was like, oh my God, the smell. It smelt so good. It smelt like the markets at home, it even smelt like my momma's kitchen.' Every which way he turned, he said, the smells kept on coming. 'Sometimes I would just walk into a shop just for the smell and then walk out again,' he says, chuckling at the memory.

Having bought all the ingredients he had been desperately searching for and craving, he began batch-cooking a whole array of meals from home, always making sure there were enough leftovers to grab out of the fridge and reheat in the microwave at work. This plan worked out well for the guys he lived with too – as soon as they smelt what he was cooking, they were hooked. 'They were like, oh man, can we try this? Then they'd ask what I was cooking tomorrow.' It sounds like he was helping them fill a home-cooking induced homesickness hole too.

Getting this taste felt like 'magic', he says. 'When you don't have something that you've been used to for years – you've had it so much so that it's in your blood, then in a shot it's gone – your body will feel like, "What's going on?"' He didn't feel whole without his food from home, he says; he felt like his body was missing something, but when it returned, 'magical' is the word he repeats again. He says his body felt stronger, he felt more like himself again.

The connection we all have to food is inescapable. Not everyone is lucky enough to grow up in a house where fresh food is prepared, not every parent likes to cook, not every parent has the time to cook, and of course not every parent *can* cook. So not everyone grows up in a home where the smell of freshly cooked food brings back a multitude of beautiful memories. But the thing about the connection between food and home is that it doesn't always *have* to be about the physical act of smelling our parents' cooking; sometimes it's just about smelling food which reminds us of the taste of home.

It's like being in foreign holiday resorts that insist on serving British Sunday roasts, or a full English breakfast. Sometimes British holidaymakers just want the taste and smell of home, even though it invariable *never* tastes the same as home. Trust me, I've done it a million times. Instead, it's sort of, I dunno, home-adjacent or something. But sometimes, that in itself is enough, and will just have to do.

Food, though, is one of three branches of the tree that Moses believes are essential to feeling grounded when you're away from home. Especially almost ten thousand kilometres away, as he was. 'The first branch is the food, number two is the music because that's the only thing that you can definitely get from home, and number three is connecting with someone from home.' He explains that you can meet someone new who's from home and immediately there's a connection; and if you meet regularly – say, once a week – it can be enough to keep you going no matter where you are in the world, when your heart aches from so much unfamiliarity.

'If you have the food, if you have the music, if you have the community, then you feel complete. Then you feel at home.' Of this he is very sure.

But no sooner had he finally completed the three branches

of his tree, a spanner was thrown into the works. He fell in love with a woman that he wanted to spend the rest of his life with. But she was from London. They married, and the decision was made to move to London.

Moses was then forced to start putting together the three branches of his tree in a place that was, once again, very different to the one before.

He moved six months ago and describes London and Dubai as being the complete opposite of each other: 'Dubai is never-ending. It has a twenty-four-hour cycle. It's non-stop, even at night. You can come out of your house and go anywhere and do anything whether it's 8 p.m. or 3 a.m. It's a different lifestyle. It's always busy.' But then he moved to London, 'and everything closed at 5 o'clock'. Yep, it was an adjustment. 'I'm trying to reset, it's like opening a new folder that says I live in London now, and I'm still trying to navigate it.'

But you can tell he's homesick again – that the small hole in the pit of his stomach he had in those first few months in Dubai is back, and he so desperately wants to close it again. So, he has begun to use the skills he used last time round to build his three branches, since it worked so well the last time. He recently met up with a friend from Nigeria who he hadn't seen in three years, and the beginnings of one of the branches are starting to grow.

As for the food part, that's where his wife comes into play. She's of Indian origin and was absolutely convinced that if there was anywhere Moses could find the ingredients he needed for his meals, it would be London, one of the most ethnically diverse cities in the world. Moses was wary of not finding the exact ingredients he needed, but she assured him it would be fine, and convinced him there was no need to pack his suitcase full of the spices from the Nigerian supermarkets in Dubai. What she hadn't accounted for was how specific her husband was about the spices he uses – they had to be from a particular brand that's not that easily available here. There are loads of alternatives, but for Moses, they would alter the taste and smell, and he yearned for something exactly the same. Plus people kept suggesting shops that specialised in ingredients for *North* African dishes, and anyone who has tasted food from Morocco and Nigeria will know the taste spectrums are very different.

That's where I came into the story of Moses – his wife WhatsApped me to ask if I knew where he'd be able to find the ingredients he needed anywhere near their house. Yes, there is *some* crossover between Caribbean and West African food – one came from the other, obviously. But on the whole, the base of the spice blends that are used for both tend to be slightly dissimilar. However, I knew the areas where he was more likely to find this very important and *very* specific ingredient he needed (it's a powdered chicken-flavoured stock by a brand called Benny). I completely understood why he was determined to complete the mission; he's been far from home a long time, and he needed those tastes and smells to help settle his soul.

They travelled to the areas I'd suggested and he eventually found the shops he needed, but they still didn't have this one ingredient. He then jumped on Google and started making calls, and found what seems like the *only* place in London to stock it. But the shopkeeper had run out, and promised to bring some back in three weeks on her next trip to Nigeria.

They exchanged numbers and, incredibly heart-warmingly, she called him from Nigeria weeks later to find out what else he needed from home. She bought boxes of stuff back for him to buy, all of which he now has stuffed away in his kitchen cupboards. He has the biggest smile on his face as he recalls this moment, clearly over the moon that he'd completed the mission he so desperately needed to solve. 'Now I cook the food like my mom would cook.'

In fact, his wife sent me a video of the first meal he'd cooked with his much-wanted spices. And, my goodness, if I could have jumped into my phone and joined them for dinner, I would have.

What about the other branch of the tree? 'Oh, that's easy,' he says, his belly laugh returning again. 'Spotify.'

He compares the three branches of his tree to a map of Nigeria. 'It's like three branches,' he explains, 'the River Niger, and the River Benue, and then they meet in the middle,' creating another branch. If you get a chance to take a look at a map of Nigeria you'll realise he's absolutely right. When you compare the visual of that to the way he describes what you've got to do to successfully adjust to being a Nigerian living away from home, it really does hit my heart. It's quite simply beautiful.

He sees his original home of Nigeria like a tree, and that wherever he goes is an extension of that tree: another branch. You never lose that connection to home, he explains, because whatever you build elsewhere will sustain you. Because it's connected. 'You need that,' he says, 'so that you don't lose touch of where you're from. So that you don't lose yourself.'

It's a connection he wants to ensure that their children

have in the future. He wants to make sure that they under-stand the country of their father's birth, so that they feel a connection which will give them a stronger understanding of who they are, and where home is.

That connection is something I have, and is something for which I will be grateful to my parents and grandparents for, for ever. My soul will always feel connected to two places, because, to use Moses' analogy, Jamaica is where their tree began. It sprouted branches when they moved, and another when they had their children. I may live thousands of miles away, but that connection to my homeland has never dimmed, and I'm fiercely protective of that. I'm protective of both sides of me in a way that automatically comes from having parents who are from somewhere else. Because *they* are protective.

It's a protectiveness that Yue'er (we're using pseudonyms) feels towards the place of her birth: Beijing, the capital of China. Now in London with her husband Feng and two children, they both feel it's important that their children not only have a connection to China, but also *feel* that connection.

She first moved to the UK for university back in 2000, when she was eighteen, like so many Chinese students have done over the years. The boom began in the late 1990s when there was an increase in the number of middle-income families in China who could afford to send their children abroad to study. Every year around 700,000 Chinese students leave to study abroad[4] and it's a trend that continues to grow. In 2021–2022, China sent a record 151,690 students to the UK to study – more than any other country or alliance, and that includes the European Union.[5] The UK is seen as a 'safe' option in terms of international higher-education options, and of course there's the prestige of having a child who has studied here. But there has also been a rise in the teaching of English in China which has increased the affinity young students may feel they have with the UK and America. Though for many, the UK is seen as the safer option of the two, with less geopolitical tension.

As a student in the UK, Yue'er missed her friends, her family, and the food from the place of her birth hugely. 'I'm not talking about the posh food, I mean the day-to-day sort of Chinese cuisine.' By this, she doesn't mean the Chinese takeaways that pepper villages and towns up and down the UK (and which originated in Hong Kong); she means the vastly different variety of dishes that she grew up with in Beijing. To Brits, the two may seem interchangeable, but the reality is they're very much not.

Hong Kong food is heavily influenced by British food, thanks to the city becoming a British colonial outpost back in 1841. Like so many of the British colonial influences globally, Hong Kong food is a fusion of British preferences and native tastes. So much of it is put down to the collision of cultures: egg tart, milk tea, and pancakes, to name a few. It was created from British meals, using Chinese ingredients – and it's this melding of Eastern and Western influences that makes Hong Kong quite unique.

The city was born out of the clash between China and Britain over opium: British and other Western traders were illegally importing it into China. That in turn sparked the outbreak of the First Opium War in 1839; by 1841 China surrendered the island to the British and an agreement called the Treaty of Nanking was signed, making the area officially a British colony. This lasted from 1841 to 1941, and again from 1945 to 1997.

The 1880s and 1890s were the heyday of colonialism in Asia, and the colonial society in Hong Kong was a direct reflection of that – especially through its food. The fusion of Chinese and British food in the upper classes of society filtered down to the working classes, and, in turn, became the food of Hong Kong. Added to that are influences of Japanese, Korean and south-east Asian cuisines due to the way the British used the port in Hong Kong. This is the Chinese food that Hong Kong Chinese brought with them to the UK after the 1948 Nationality Act allowed them, like many other immigrants, to move to the UK free of restrictions.[6,7,8]

During the 1950s and 1960s there was an increase in the Hong Kong Chinese community in the UK, with many of the newcomers going into the restaurant business and setting up takeaways. Hong Kong-born British entrepreneur Woon Wing Yip has spoken at length about the reasons for the way in which Chinese restaurants cemented themselves within British culture. He had previously mentioned the gap in the market Chinese restaurateurs found: British pubs closed between 10.30 and 11 p.m., but at the time, there was nowhere open that late to fill the hunger gap after a night of drinking. In flew Chinese takeaways to fill this space, opening until 11.30 p.m. 'We came at the right time, in the right place and do it right.'[9]

The advantage, of course, was that the food had already been adapted to British tastes under colonialism. However, further tweaks were needed for UK takeaway food at that time, to satisfy a new generation unaccustomed to (at that point) so-called 'foreign' foods.

It's not that dissimilar to the food created in Jamaica as

a result of the British colonial tastes, and the influences they brought with them to the colonies. My beloved patty is thought to have been created as a direct result of the Cornish pasty – which is of course made from meat and potato. The Jamaican love of sweet treats like Easter buns is thought to have developed because of the British sweet tooth. Interestingly, when Yue'er talks about the differences in the foods of Beijing and Hong Kong, she talks of the fact that Hong Kong food tends to be sweeter too. That, presumably, is also due to the British influence.

But Yue'er grew up almost two thousand kilometres away, in Beijing, which is why the Chinese food she found in the UK was so unfamiliar to her, and just made her miss home even more when she first arrived. With the food of Beijing having no colonial influences, it resulted in, one could argue, a more 'traditional' style of Chinese food – which is what she recognises. It involves ingredients and traditional ways of cooking that go back thousands of years, having been passed down through the generations. With no colonial interferences, it was able to preserve its history and its food. Unsurprisingly, knowing the typical British palate of the time, Hong Kong food tends to be less spicy, involving a lot less pepper, and sweeter. Chinese food? Totally the opposite, far spicier. But its history too involves a coming together of cultures and traditions.

In the seventh century, Muslim communities began to settle in Beijing and brought with them halal dishes. In the Southern Song Dynasty from 1127–1279, the Jurchen people founded a capital in Beijing, followed by the Mongols, and over the years different types of cuisines flowed through

Beijing and coexisted. During Emperor Yongle's reign as the third emperor of the Ming Dynasty (from 1402 to 1424), he made Beijing the capital of his princedom, with chefs from South China bringing with them famous dishes from the area; and at this point, the imperial dishes began to take shape. The Qing Dynasty followed (from 1644 to 1911), with the cooking methods of the Manchu people – who were based in north-east Asia – spreading to Beijing. The ebb and flow of Beijing over the centuries led to, by the late Qing Dynasty period, distinct traditions, methods and dishes which formed a Peking style, very individual in its tastes and features.[10]

Beijing was the capital city for the Liao, Jin, Yuan, Ming and Qing dynasties, all of whom (except for the Ming Dynasty) had rulers who hailed from the northern nomadic tribes. Therefore, the dishes tended to be dominated by meat dishes. The Mongolian rulers of the Yuan Dynasty (1271–1368) loved mutton, and many of those dishes are still made today (like stewed mutton, boiled mutton, fried mutton tripe, etc.).

But rather than Hong Kong, whose more modern food influences were flown in by colonisers who hailed from ten thousand kilometres away, in places like Beijing, culinary influences came from within China. Beijing was a gathering place for authors, poets, scholars and others, and with them came chefs who aided the complex flavours of modern Beijing cuisine: food from Shandong, Huai-Yang, and Jiangsu-Zhejiang were all an influence.[11]

Yue'er's family also cook more with rice than noodles, a staple which North China produced very little of until relatively recently. Many Chinese meals are served with plain steamed white rice; conversely dim sum and noodles tend to be the side dishes of choice in Hong Kong. Hong Kong's colonial connections and its food being more palatable to a British consumer accelerated its prevalence in the UK, more so than its Chinese counterpart. Which is why, when Yue'er moved to the UK and had a yearning for home and Chinese food, it was difficult to find in restaurants and takeaways here. As a result, the only way she could experience it was if she prepared it from scratch at home, especially good old traditional Pekinese hotpot – the Chinese name for which is Huo Guo, which translates to 'fire pot' in English, and FYI it's nothing like a traditional British hotpot as favoured by the diners in *Coronation Street*'s Rovers Return.

The dish is made using pots made of copper or clay, with a chimney that rises in the middle of it. It holds the coal that you light which then heats the pot. Broth is added to the pot which produces a ring around the chimney, then various raw ingredients are added like meat, vegetables, and dumplings. Served with rice (or noodles) on the side, it's a communal dish. 'Back when I was little, that's what we would have for family gatherings and for special occasions,' Yue'er says. Her family didn't have much money back then, so the dish was preserved for things like Chinese New Year. That and Peking Duck, she says, were real treats that she would really look forward to as a child.

Back when she first moved to the UK, the smells and cooking traditions from home were few and far between. Now, though, there are chain restaurants in the UK called Haidilao which specialise in Chinese hotpots; it's the largest hotpot chain in China, with three in London that she often frequents with her family when she wants a taste of home.

She says she fell in love with the UK as soon as she arrived. Straight from the airport, she headed to Wales to spend time in the countryside, ahead of starting at university in Reading. And though her heart remained in China, there were aspects of this new country that reminded her of home. 'Growing up in Beijing, I was fortunate enough to live in a house with a garden. We had slugs, and I played with the snails, we had lawns, and little plum trees. Then we moved to an apartment block.' Their accommodation was high up, so all the joy she had gleaned from the beautiful garden that sat right outside her house was gone.

But it was during her rambles through the Welsh countryside that she realised how much she had missed those early years of her life. She also realised that she was already beginning to grow an attachment to this land that was thousands of miles away from the home where she was raised. An attachment which grew after she moved into student halls. 'I guess it was my little home. But it depends on what we define as home, doesn't it?' She says that for her, it was her base. One that gave her a sense of security. But she missed her family terribly. The four walls of her student home kept her safe, she says, but it wasn't home without her family. She made good girlfriends who almost felt like sisters, a type of family of sorts. But it wasn't quite the real thing. And there was a big part of her that was aching for that.

It wasn't until she married and had her first child, Arthur (now eleven years old), that her emotions started to shift. 'It made me feel like, oh, maybe this is now my home.' She recalls a light-bulb moment for her with a former boss: 'I worked for him back in 2007 and then he went on secondment. He came back in 2010 and was like, "Oh girl, you

British now!"' She laughs, remembering how the conversation took her aback at the time. 'But I think when I started working I was more Chinese.'

The question of whether or not she was more British or Chinese had never really crossed her mind before then. She just felt she was very fortunate to have been given the chance to leave China and have a different kind of life to others that she had grown up alongside back in Beijing. 'My mum sent me here. She was of that generation that would send their children abroad to study.' As a family they had talked about the options, especially since her grandfather had studied at Cambridge as an exchange student many years prior. So the family felt an affinity to the UK, and it had been her mum's dream that one day she too would leave home and follow in her father's footsteps.

Sadly, China's Great Proletarian Cultural Revolution which took place from 1966 to 1976 ended that dream. It was a period when Communist Party chairman Mao Zedong wanted to renew the spirit of the Communist revolution and root out what he thought to be 'bourgeois' infiltrators. In 1966, he framed it as the struggle of the proletariat against the bourgeoisie, but it crippled the economy and ruined millions of lives, with intellectuals and party officials murdered or driven to suicide. It triggered a decade of turmoil, bloodshed, hunger and stagnation.

Eventually the country's rulers concluded that the entire ten-year episode had been a disaster that had gifted the country with little but disorder and damage. The party called it 'the most severe setback and the heaviest losses suffered by the party, by the country, and the people since the founding of the People's Republic'.[12]

Thanks to the revolution ending the hopes of Yue'er's mother to study abroad and potentially create a new home elsewhere, the dream then fell to the next in line, her daughter. 'My mother always had this regret in her mind,' she concludes. When Yue'er was in high school, her mother decided that she was not going to complete her education in China, especially as a girl. She felt her daughter would have far more opportunity to thrive if she left home.

It's a decision made by many Chinese parents and their daughters when it comes to studying abroad. A five-year Australian study by Fran Martin looked into why, and found that the reasons had two main strands. In the first were students' and families' worries about the increasing gender discrimination among employers, with many in the private sector not willing to hire women in their twenties for fear that they'll run off, get married, and have children. An oversees degree qualification would give them an advantage over male graduates in the job market.

In the second strand were those who fell into the 'leftover women' category: those slightly older women students (late twenties) who wanted to have a fair amount of distance from the pressures to get married and have children, because of the stigma of being 'leftover'. Many parents want to give their daughters more choices in their life, rather than have them feel trapped in a future of marriage and babies and stalled careers which they have no control over. Sending them abroad gives them a certain level of control over their futures. Education is a big reason why so many immigrants choose to build their homes elsewhere.[13]

My maternal grandad was a huge stickler for education;

he was strict with my mum and her siblings when it came to making sure they got a good education. He pushed them all, hard. Part of his reasoning for taking up the cry for help from the British government after the Second World War was because he saw it as an opportunity for a better life for his family, especially his children. He felt they could achieve far more if they made that trip across the Atlantic Ocean, and therefore improve the future of the generations that would follow. It's a trend which has continued for generations of immigrants – the lure of the UK and the chance of better prospects there.

As Yue'er boarded the plane to leave the only home she'd ever known, she packed the thing that meant the most to her at the time: a picture of her family. Technology was in a very different place back then: no video calls on your phone or computer, just phone calls. She brought the picture of her family so that she could see their faces in those moments when she missed being with them at home. Visas were hard to secure, and so they weren't able to visit her to remind her of home in person. Instead they would send gifts through friends and business contacts who were visiting the UK.

Sometimes it would be food that her family knew she missed, and at times her dad would send her handwritten letters which, she says, would inevitably make her cry. The yearning for home was made stronger because she knew by then that he was ill, and it hurt both her heart and her body to not be able to be physically with him. To hug him. To hold his hand. 'I think he was trying to make sure that I knew he was fine. He would always tell me to make the most of my time here and not to worry about home.' Her voice becomes quieter, and shakier, as the memories of her dad start flooding back.

She talks to me about the mid-autumn festival, or the Moon Festival, in Chinese culture. It's one of the most important holidays in the Chinese calendar and is held on the fifteenth day of the eighth lunar month. This generally runs from 23 August to 23 September on our calendar, and always falls in the middle of the autumn season in China. It's the time of the year when the moon is believed to be at its fullest and brightest. It symbolises reunion, and is the time when families appreciate the moon together. There's a well-known poem that's associated with the festival, written by Su Shi (one of China's greatest poets and essayists). The final few lines are:

> The moon should bear us no grudge, why is it oft full
>   and bright when people part from each other?
> People may have sorrows and joys, partings and
>   reunions, as well as the moon is bright or dim, wax
>   and wane. Rare is perfect since the ancient time
> May we live long and share the beauty of the moon
>   together, even if we are hundreds of miles apart.

Yue'er tells me that it's the final line of the poem that her dad would write down in letters to her. Telling her, 'No matter where you are, you're looking at the same full moon. It's the same full moon.' She begins to cry at the beautiful memories bestowed on her by her father, and the culture that allowed them both to still feel connected.

Her dad had been diagnosed with cancer not long after

she left for the UK. She suspects he wasn't feeling great long before she boarded the plane but didn't want to ruin his daughter's chance of something great, so he kept it to himself. About a week after she left came the diagnosis. Her parents didn't tell her until much later.

Her dad becoming ill while she was being given this incredible opportunity because of *their* hard work impacted her. She also realised what her mum was having to juggle at home. 'They paved the way for me to come here. But then my mum was under so much pressure; she carried so much extra burden.' In the years after her father's passing, she told Yue'er that several people had been pushing her at the time to bring her daughter, her only child, back home. Their community was aghast that she wasn't forcing Yue'er to return to China to help carry the burden, but according to Yue'er, 'she kept telling them, "My daughter has her future, and that future is that country." She told her daughter repeatedly to stay in the UK.

Yue'er was oblivious to all this at the time. Her mum shielded her from what was happening at home so that her daughter would be able to enjoy the chance of a new life that she never had. 'I felt like I was blessed,' Yue'er says.

She felt a sense of calm when she came here, compared to what she calls the 'Super City' of Beijing, where rapid development meant large swathes of building work and high population numbers. As she walked the streets around her new home, she would marvel at the fact that everyone was just so nice: 'Super, super nice, and in my mind, I thought I'd love to be one of them, you know – happy and smiling. But still working hard.'

She was still at university when her dad passed away. Her

parents had worked so hard to give their daughter a life they could never have had, and although her dad saw the first flutters of that new life developing, he wasn't able to see it truly grow. 'After I graduated, my mum told me to go for a job in the UK. She told me not to come back.' Yue'er and her dad had had a strong connection, and her mum felt it would be too hard for her daughter to come back home and try to adjust to a life without him there. 'She said that I was now on my own and I should make the best of my life here.' She credits her mum's strength for making sure she didn't veer from the path that her parents had set out for her.

It's a path that Yue'er has continued with her own children, eleven-year-old Arthur and four-year-old Anne. The family has recently moved house, so the memorabilia like little Chinese charms that Yue'er would usually have adorning the walls are still packed away in boxes. But she does make sure the children hear Chinese music in the house regularly. Arthur, though, has shown little interest despite his mum trying routinely to cajole him into listening to it. Conversely, Anne, who is definitely the more confident and outspoken of the two, is 'more open-minded when I put on Chinese pop songs'.

The family moved to Hong Kong for a few years for Feng's job, and Arthur attended an international school, where he would try to perform Chinese songs in school plays. It's easy to tell that those moments would fill Yue'er with pride at the connection her son was developing to the country of her birth. Back in the UK, both children attend Mandarin school once a week for two hours. 'Arthur can now read and write the language to a near native level.' She admits to pushing him hard, and that's why he is now so good at it. 'He knows it's a good language to hold on to, so we make him stay on track.'

There's clearly more to being part of a culture than speaking the language fluently. For this family, Mandarin is a useful language for Arthur to be proficient in as a global language of the future. Many think that Mandarin may well replace English as the language that's most impactful in the world. China's economic prowess is ever-growing, so it would make sense. But it's not an easy language to get your head around, so for those who can, it is a huge advantage. Yue'er's children being fluent in the language of their parents is also connected to family and home. I was fortunate enough to meet Yue'er's mum quite a few times, as she's in London at the moment to spend time with the family for a few weeks. Our conversations involved me flailing my hands around in a feeble attempt at communication, because she does not speak English and I don't speak Mandarin. If her grandchildren also didn't speak or understand Mandarin, it would create a huge chasm in their relationship which would cause disappointment on both sides.

The children being able to communicate effectively with the wider family in the first language of both their parents adds to the multitude of intertwining layers of what it means to know your roots, and the importance of what home means. Without those roots, how can an individual effectively stand tall and proud? This is what sits ever-present in the background of the reasons why Yue'er pushes them so hard to understand their culture. 'Come on!' she emphatically tells me. 'They can't lose their roots. They are 100 per cent Chinese by blood, and they must recognise that. And luckily, they are very proud of it. Which they should be.'

She feels it's important because in the Western world they will come across racist comments, and being proud of where they come from will provide them with the armour they need to survive those comments. It's as though their strong identity will add weight to their superpowers. From experience, it's a sentiment that I completely agree with.

It's also a superpower which Arthur needed when they returned from Hong Kong and he attended a birthday party after enrolling in a new school. 'Arthur was one of the only non-white children at the party, all aged eight and nine years old, and they started making fun of the fact that he was darker than the others.' One of the other mums who was there, who is of Asian heritage, was horrified and let Yue'er know what had happened. She raised it with the school, and they, in turn, attempted to educate the kids about equality and diversity. Although, I'm consistently of the opinion that schools should be proactive rather than reactive, which would cause fewer ethnic minority kids to find themselves in such heartbreaking situations. But that's a whole other book in itself.

Out of everyone I've spoken to for this book, Yue'er is the first to talk about the way in which the British values system has impacted her, and how it played a part in moulding the grown-up that she became. When she came here, she says, 'I started to appreciate things, and build my value system. And I think I've got a lot of good things out of the [British] system because of that.' From that grew a deep-seated love for the country, the home which raised her to become an adult. 'People ask me, do you see yourself as British? Do you see yourself as Chinese? I think I see myself as British-Chinese. I love these two countries, and if there's anything I could do to make those two countries happy, I would do that. I feel like I get the most out of both.'

They fly to Beijing regularly to visit her mum in order to keep that connection alive, but would she return home for ever? 'As much as I would love to, I don't think the political system is friendly towards us. Both my and my husband Feng's mums get judged because we are living overseas. Twenty years ago, when General Hu Jintao was president, it was more open-minded, more welcoming.'

Yue'er has mentioned frequently during our conversation about keeping hold of the thread that pulls her towards the culture of the home she was raised in, and talked about how much she missed her parents when she moved to the UK. But, interestingly, she's mentioned very little about how much she misses her home, as in China itself. But perhaps that's tied into the changes the country has been through which means the pull back home doesn't have the same intensity, unlike with my father.

China has gone through a lot over the years under the watchful eye of the Chinese Communist Party, the ruling political party which founded the People's Republic of China in 1949. Since then, the country has witnessed rapid economic growth, and the world has seen it grow as a global power. However, the party's decisions, especially those of its current leader Xi Jinping, haven't gone down well with everyone at home or abroad. In particular, its human rights violations have come under intense scrutiny and criticism. Under that list comes silencing dissent, restricting the rights and freedoms of citizens and censorship. Yet, some call Xi Jinping the most influential leader since Mao.

Yue'er is very honest and matter of fact. 'Do I miss home when I'm here? No, not so much.' But then comes the curveball.

'The moment I land in Beijing, that smell of the air immediately draws me in, all the way back home. Oh, and it's a magic smell!' she excitedly tells me with such incredible warmth it's infectious. 'To some people I know, it smells bad. It smells polluted or whatever that is. But I love it. It's my childhood smell, from the moment I come out of the airport.'

I know from experience that when I step off the plane in Jamaica it hits my heart in a way I can sometimes struggle to explain, so I ask her if it hits hers too. She erupts, 'YES! YES! YES! 100 per cent!' But, she explains, it doesn't hit in a way that makes her yearn for it; that feeling has metamorphosed and changed over time. It's something different altogether – she now thinks of and describes China as her 'distant home'.

'It's not my home,' she says, 'it's my mum's home. I mean, yes it's my home. But it's not *my* home. That home is London, where I live with *my* family.'

The change happened when they had their first child, and she realised that she really was laying roots elsewhere. 'I feel like there are different levels to it. The highest level that made it really clear that this is our home path was when we had children.'

She's absolutely right, of course – there are so many levels to the debate over where we think of as home, and that *can* change over time due to so many different factors. Children can be one of the biggest of these factors, but it can go either way. There are those whose pull back home becomes even stronger once they have children, and they want them to share in the type of environment that they were raised in. I have many friends who've made the move away from London and back home to less hectic (and expensive) parts of the UK because they want them to have a childhood similar to the one they experienced. Others, like Yue'er, develop an affinity with their new surroundings, with little interest in returning.

My maternal aunt, Eleanor, is the same. Unlike my uncle, her brother, she never harboured intentions to head back 'home' in her retirement years. That thread was never as strong for her, it didn't grab hold of her in the same way emotionally. She is undeniably connected to her roots, it's very much a part of who she is – which helped to strengthen our link to it. It's a scenario which is very similar with my paternal aunts, those which were born in Jamaica, who never moved back. My paternal uncle, Vassel, though, always had it as part of his life plan, and he was able to live out his final days in the land of his birth. Just as he wanted it.

When you move countries to a new home there is no one homogenous way to think or feel about it. Despite my paternal grandma being a fiercely proud Jamaican, she had absolutely zero intention of moving back. London was her home, and she lived a good life surrounded by friends and family. She lived out her dying days here, in the same house that she'd lived in for decades. That was her home, and that's what made her happy.

Chapter 4

Fleeing War

Families fleeing war zones and conflict has become a steady feature not just of the past century, but throughout history. The displacement of millions of families due to situations they have no control over, means them having to leave their homes and their relatives, often at short notice, in order to keep themselves, and their families, safe. A life that you could have spent years building can disappear at the flick of a switch, with no idea of what your future holds or where exactly the road will lead you – or even if you'll stay alive long enough to reach the as yet unknown destination. The home which had once kept you safe is no longer able to guarantee your survival in the face of the might of the machines of war.

The UN Refugee Agency describes a refugee as someone who has been forced to flee their country because of persecution, war or violence. War, and ethnic, tribal and religious violence are the leading causes of refugees fleeing their countries. Fifty-two per cent of all refugees and others who need international protection come from just three countries: Syria,

Ukraine, and Afghanistan. At the end of 2022, 108.4 million people had been forcibly displaced worldwide, 35.3 million of whom were refugees (figures from the UNHCR) Of that number, 5.7 million came from Ukraine, 174,000 of whom moved to the UK under the Ukraine Family Scheme, and the Ukraine Sponsorship Scheme.

In the UK we only hear a snapshot of the true number of those who've been forced to leave the place that they have called home. Yes, the top three are from Syria, Ukraine, and Afghanistan – conflicts which most British people are well aware of. But focusing just on those countries doesn't give a true picture of the instability that's happening globally on a daily basis. Below that top three list you can add those fleeing from Venezuela, because of years of political and economic instability; South Sudan, because of ongoing conflicts and natural disasters (figures from World Vision); and Myanmar, due to the Rohingya people fleeing violence, persecution and human rights violations.

Families the world over are having to take to the road with very little and try to find somewhere they can lay their head and call home. In the midst of the rhetoric that's often woven into the debate regarding immigration and refugees, *what* someone is fleeing from is often lost. But the reality is that no one would put their children through the trauma of travelling across the world for safety, if they have any sort of choice. Choosing to live or be persecuted is not a choice anyone would take on voluntarily. But what happens to the way you think of your home when you are forced to leave it?

That is what millions of Ukrainians were forced to do when Russia's President Putin restarted his invasion attempts in February 2022. Controlling the country has been on the president's bucket list for quite some time; he's tried repeatedly to force the country to bend to his way of thinking for the past two decades. Putin doesn't accept that the country has its own separate national identity; instead he believes it *is* and *should be* a part of Russia. Bringing Ukraine back into the Russian fold is a throwback to how things used to be, prior to the Soviet Union breaking up in 1991. But it's not just about nostalgia, it's about land . . . as so many of these situations are. Ukraine in central to his plans for pushing back the growing expansion of NATO. He physically needs Ukraine, to be able to achieve his goal of influence around Russia's western borders. Plus, a Western-orientated and successful nation like Ukraine is a great advert for the alternative life the Russian people *could* be living, an alternative its leader desperately wants hidden from them. But central to this entire episode are families who don't want to be caught up in the whims of a leader craving more power.

Families like husband and wife Oleksandr (known as Alex) Mulyak and Yuliia Polikovska, two of more than 8 million Ukrainian refugees who, since 15 February 2023, almost a year after the war in Ukraine began, have been registered in Europe. This represents 18 per cent of their country's population. The majority of those border crossings happened in March 2022 – within weeks of the war starting. Alex, Yuliia, their young children Lev and Ahata, and Yuliia's mum were part of that first wave. Yuliia, her mum and the children went first, with Alex following three months later. Their journey to safety took them via Vienna, until it finally ended, months after they originally left, in

London. The family are now able to have some semblance of stability, with Lev in school and Ahata in pre-school. At the same time, they're being constantly updated on the progress of the resistance against Russia and President Putin through TV channels, online, and through those who were not able to leave.

Left behind was a home that they had spent eight years building for their family, says Yuliia. They didn't have enough money to employ builders for the final steps, so they did a lot themselves, including putting in flooring and painting walls. Just the two of them. They'd made it into a space that worked for all of them and their love for the outdoors. 'Our family home was very big and close to a big park. Almost every day, the four of us would go walking in the forest, picking up mushrooms and playing with our dog.'

The space outside their home, she says, was used to create a green space full of different plants and fruits, including berries and grapes. 'Everyone had their own corner in our house, a space for activities and for reading a book in a quiet atmosphere.' Both Yuliia and Alex clearly have so much pride in the little corner of Ukraine that they built. They share anecdotes of trying to manage the build while both working full-time, finishing their jobs at 6 p.m. then going straight to the house to carry on the work.

Alex laughs when he tells the story of ordering a play-tower to keep the kids occupied in the garden. When it arrived, the quality wasn't great so he sent it straight back the same day. But Alex is not one to let a stumbling block to get in the way of a plan, so he went out and bought some wood and built a play-tower himself. The joy the family clearly gleaned from the outdoors extended to the water too, with Alex opening a sailing school with a friend a few years ago. Lev quickly learnt to love the open water too. 'We spent a lot of time on the water. He loved sailing,' Alex remembers.

The home the family built was one they intended to raise their family in, filled with love. The joy they got from it and the connection they had to it is obvious from the way they talk about it. It threads constantly through the conversation. The life they had, though, is worlds apart from life they have been thrust into in London. As they talk about their big house with all this outdoor space on the outskirts of a forest in Lviv, I glance around the small house they now live in, in the suburbs of London. 'I miss that space now I'm here,' admits Yuliia. It's safe, yes, but this corner of London didn't feature in their original plan for the future of raising their family. *That* plan was shattered by a man who lived just over a thousand kilometres from their home in Moscow. A man they had never met, but who had the ability and the power to change the entire course of their lives. Like so many leaders have done to so many families, in so many parts of the world, over far too many centuries.

They finished building their home a year before the war started. But then came 24 February 2022, when the tectonic plates of their lives shifted, causing an earthquake of emotions which left them having to make one of the biggest, and yet easiest decisions for the sake of their family.

Having never lived through or experienced war first-hand, especially one in a social media age, I'm not sure what I expected in terms of the start of an invasion. But the calmness with which they both talk about it beginning just makes it all the more heartbreaking. When you've travelled two thousand miles, and started your life again, perhaps the magnitude of what sparked the fear and the fleeing is overshadowed by the need to just get your family to safety.

The family were asleep at home in their beds when war began: Yuliia, Alex, their children, and both their mums. All had gone to bed not knowing that the following morning their country would be under attack, and that a peaceful night's sleep in those beds were coming swiftly to an end. All were blind to what was ahead, unlike the man who started this war. His final night at home in the hours before dropping bombs on innocent Ukrainians must have been very different. But who knows, maybe he too had a peaceful night's sleep?

Russian forces began their bombardment at dawn, and they went all-in: troops took to the ground, accompanied by air and missile strikes. One day those strikes reached Lviv, which is located in the west of Ukraine, one of the furthest points away from the border of Russia. The strike fell one kilometre away from Yuliia and Alex's home, on the road they would take daily to Lev's school. The close proximity of the strikes on that first day was the catalyst for a series of events that would change any plans they may have had for the future of their family and their home.

Alex remembers that morning clearly. It wasn't the sound or the impact of missiles that tipped him off that something was amiss, it was WhatsApp. 'At 5.30 in the morning, I got the first message in my work group chat.' In Ukraine, Alex was a product manager for a software development company (he has a PhD in Engineering). His team were scattered around various parts of the country, and when the first bombs were dropped the messages started flying in from those who could hear, and feel, the explosions: from Kharkiv in the east (nearer to the Russian border), Kyiv (more towards the middle of the country) and Dnipro (also more towards the east), to name a few. A picture was emerging that showed that this attack was not just concentrated in one area of the country – it was a coordinated, widespread attack that sent the message that no area was completely safe.

But then the sound of war arrived within earshot of their home. First came the sound of the missiles, then the rumbling sensation that swiftly followed, indicating they had struck the ground, destroying an area nearby that they knew well. Alex and Yuliia had no idea if the next strike would edge even closer to their home, and they did not know if their family would last the day. They had no clue as to whether or not, as a family, they had just spent their final night together. If they had known, would they have done anything differently the night before? Who knows.

The couple consider themselves one of the lucky ones because they had a basement in their home, so the family decamped there for the day and a night. There, the important task was keeping a one-year-old and a four-year-old occupied, without showing them just how scared the grown-ups were. The adults decided the basement would help mask the sounds of the destruction that was playing out in real time outside, 'Just so they could understand that they were safe,' says Yuliia.

Alex kept popping up to the living room to keep an eye

on the sounds of war, to work out how close their home was to possible destruction. The second strike he heard was four kilometres away, at the local electricity station. But the decision had already been made: fearful of losing his entire family in the conflict, he knew they needed to get out. 'I told [Yuliia] that I don't know what will happen tomorrow, but for me it would be easier to manage myself without you and the kids.' So began the swift process of packing for a destination which was as yet unknown, with no idea whether they were packing for weeks, months or years, or whether they'd ever return to their home, or the country of their birth.

The process of the couple's decision to leave, and their eventual departure, reminds me of the beautiful poem by the award-winning British-Somalian writer Warsan Shire, called 'Home'. Capturing the perils of leaving when you have no other choice, it puts me in mind of the reality of Yuliia's journey – she had no idea where she was going. It was impossible to know at that point. But anywhere was going to be safer than home. I think it's important to think about it in the terms which Warsan has described it. Home for so many is a place where we can seek solace, and where we ought to feel safe. But when that home is dangerous, it is heartbreaking. And yet once that decision is made, the journey to some semblance of safety begins.

As Yuliia began the process of deciding what to leave behind and what to take, Alex called and messaged friends to work out which border they should head for. The decision the family made to leave home was one that millions of Ukrainian families made at the same time, who all began the process of packing up what they could and trying every possible mode of transport to get out, to safety. With so many people all trying to leave at exactly the same time, the borders became chaotic, and the potential waiting times soon reached four days. It just wasn't feasible. So while Alex looked at other options, Yuliia concentrated on working out what she, her mother and the children would need.

'For me it was just a bag of clothes; that [part] wasn't important for me because you can always buy something. I packed the favourite toys of the kids for the car because we understood it was going to be a long way, and we didn't know where we were going.' Their legal and personal documents obviously came with them, and their jewellery – especially Yuliia's wedding ring, a pair of earrings, and a necklace, pieces that told the story of their life in Ukraine. She also grabbed pictures of the family together before destruction entered their lives. 'I took a couple of pictures from the last photo session of us.' The picture, perhaps, to remind both the grown-ups and the children of a more innocent time, before the children became victims of war.

It's not easy to decide what to take with you when you're fleeing. You don't want to waste space with the frivolous, but you do want to try to take items that you feel tied to in your heart. Especially when you're a historian like Yuliia, who knew there was a good chance that the country they were on the verge of leaving might never exist again. She wanted to make sure that they also took items that told the story of who they were, who their family were, and where they were from. History shows that a change in a regime or a change in 'ownership' of a country can signal the end of that country as it once was, with its future unknown. It would be therefore down to those who are left to tell the stories of what came before, and for Yuliia, grabbing paintings and traditional Ukrainian clothes to take with her was important.

She points to a painting on the wall near where we are talking. 'It's from the city where I was born. It's a mountain [design] with the sheep who live on the mountain. It tells the story of my motherland, of Kosiv.' Alex takes the picture off the wall so that I can take a closer look. It's about the size of an A3 sheet of paper, so not too big to slide in between boxes in the back of a car. It's black and white, with a chevron pattern covering the rear of the painting, and seven sheep etched into the top third of it. The main image is of a man on a horse. The man represents the people who live in the mountains who ride horses. The man looks like he's shepherding the sheep, while holding a shepherd's crook. Kosiv, a mountain town that sits in the west of Ukraine, is where both Yuliia and her mum were born. The name of the area comes from the indigenous people of the Carpathian Mountains, who were cattle breeders and craftsmen. And this picture was created by Yuliia's grandfather. 'He was a painter, who worked in factories making souvenirs.' This piece, though, was created for his family.

Yuliia is fiercely proud and protective of the town of her and her mother's birth, so I can completely understand why the painting was one of the important items for her to take with her. 'I know the pain of our grandparents. How hard it was for them to be Ukrainian one hundred years ago, two hundred years ago. The Russians want to kill Ukrainians just because we're Ukrainian. We just want to keep our own identity.' She continues: 'Every nation is exceptional, but we are exceptional in our traditions and our feeling of freedom. History is important.'

A big part of her heart is taken up with where her family is originally from: it's a small town that's found itself being pulled this way and that, through multiple generations, in terms of who 'owns' it. It's also an area that's seen a huge amount of loss over the years. In 1772 it was incorporated into the Habsburg Empire, so was under Austrian rule. After the First World War it was under Russian occupation and was faced with massacres. The West Ukrainian People's Republic took it over in 1918; by the following year it was subjected to Romanian occupation, a year later it was the Republic of Poland's turn. At the start of the Second World War, the Red Army took over, then in 1941 it fell into German hands. The rest, as they say, is history.

With the arrival of the Nazis came the mass killings and executions of more than half of the town's Jewish population. At the end of the war it became part of the USSR, then in 1991 it was part of Independent Ukraine.[1] I tell you this very brief look at the history of Kosiv because I think it's integral to the background of why this painting is so important. Yuliia comes from a country where they had to fight hard to maintain who her people were, in the constant onslaught of other countries trying to lay claim to its land.

It's a story that has been passed down through the generations of her mother's side of the family, so that they all understand where they come from, and can therefore have more of an understanding of who they are – along with the strength, power, and fight that lies deep inside them. The more you get to know Yuliia, the more you see glimmers of that within her too. The importance of taking this picture – keeping hold of the memory of the place of her and her mother's birth – is magnified by the fact that Yuliia's mother was in the middle of cancer treatment when war began in February 2022; and despite successfully managing to eventually restart her chemotherapy treatment during their journey to find a new home, within a year she was dead.

At this point in her retelling, the stoicism that is so evident within Yuliia begins to wobble, and she starts to cry. Her grief is still so very raw. She fought hard to keep her mum alive in the midst of fleeing the destruction at home, and for a brief time, the treatment worked. But in the end it wasn't the destruction of her country that took Yuliia's mum. Two months before Yuliia and I spoke, her mother lost a battle of a different kind: one that no amount of negotiations could prevent, one that both Yuliia and Alex were powerless to stop.

With her mum now gone, it is Yuliia who is left to tell the stories from home, with her grandfather's picture hanging on their wall acting as a visual testimonial of her family's history. Reminding the children of where they come from, of their home, is important for both Alex and Yuliia – and the trickle-down effect of that passion is visible now in six-year-old Lev. Since the first day of the war in February 2022, he made the conscious decision to keep his hair in a Oseledets style, where a long lock of hair is grown on the top of the head, with short back-and-sides for the rest of it – a style most associated with the Cossacks, the Ukrainian warriors. 'He probably feels more proud and self-confident with it,' Yuliia says, and if you were to meet Lev, you'd know that his mother has summed him up perfectly. When he arrived in the UK he spoke no English, yet that never dimmed his spirit or his confidence. He quickly picked up the language like a pro, and made friends easily and seamlessly. His confidence is incredible, showing a calm and steady persona of someone far older than his years. He's a joy to be around.

The pride both Yuliia and Alex have for their home country is definitely reflected in the items they gravitated towards in those few hours where they had to choose what to bring. For example, they packed traditional Ukrainian shirts, because they too tell the story of their country's history. As I don't know what they look like, Yuliia quickly pops upstairs to grab one so that I can see.

They're called *vyshyvanka*, which is the Ukrainian word for a shirt adorned with traditional embroidered designs. Each region in Ukraine will have a different design, and each embroiderer will have a different style and technique. Yuliia's is red and cream in colour. The neckline is round with red tassels attached, and three-quarters of both sleeves are a beautiful vibrant red, with an embroidered design created with white thread. The cuffs are a mix of embroidered colours, with red as the base colour. 'The design is probably about a hundred years old,' she informs me.

It really is a beautiful shirt, even when you don't know its history, and it fits Yuliia's frame perfectly. The colours are important on a *vyshyvanka*: white represents purity and holiness. Blue – which is usually for the men – is for protecting against disease and bringing peace of mind. Yellow is about abundance and joy. Green is for spring and youth. The children and Alex all have their own. Historically they were worn by both men and women in the villages; these days they're mostly worn for national holidays and festivals. So you can see why Yuliia wanted to make sure she took them, so that her family remained connected to the place that they were fleeing. But it's also more than that. When they drove away that day in February 2022, Yuliia had no idea if they would ever be able to return – and if they ever did, whether their house would still be standing. To lose so many parts of both their histories would have been heartbreaking.

As she talks, I notice two cushions that stood out to me when I first walked into their living room, and I realise that they too are embroidered with an intricate design. They stand out because it feels like one of few markers in the room that reflects the colourful family life that they both talk so passionately about. 'Are they from home too?' I ask. 'Yes,' she replies. 'I found them somewhere in the basement at home; they're originally from my grandma's house and were popular in the '60s and '70s. They're beautiful and remind me of home.'

Thanks to the choices they made the day they packed up, they've got pockets of home in a corner of London. It shows the strength of both parents that in the face of such uncertainty, they were certain that no matter what happened they would preserve their history. Although, Alex adds, 'I don't think it's important to have something that reminds you of home, what's more important is to survive. That's what was crucial.'

The couple first met eighteen years previously, at a Scout meeting, when Yuliia was fifteen years old and Alex was seventeen. They were both in the local Scout group, and it was Alex who plucked up the courage to make the first move.

They started talking on the bus on the way home from a big Scout event and swapped numbers. They set up a date and became a couple.

Not long afterwards, Yuliia moved to Kyiv for university, so the couple were forced to maintain a long-distance relationship for the duration of her six-year stint at uni, spending a lot of time on trains for the 1,200 kilometre journey there and back. When they tell the story it's quite beautiful really, but the commitment they had to each other at such a young age goes a long way to explaining why they made the decision to be apart for those first few months after the 2022 invasion. They knew they could survive the distance; it was just the war they had to worry about.

The day they made the decision that Yuliia, the kids and her mum would go first, they had no idea if they would be saying goodbye for ever – not just to the house they built, but to each other. At 8 p.m., two days after the bombardment began in Ukraine, the family set off, squeezed into a car packed full of belongings that they hoped would see them through. Yuliia drove the whole night to reach the border. 'I was an experienced driver in Ukraine, but it was my first experience driving in Europe on those huge roads. It was very scary, but I was responsible because I had a mission: I had two kids, I had a mum who needed treatment immediately, and I needed to find somewhere to live because all the hotels near the border were fully booked. I just needed to survive, and to settle somewhere.'

Yuliia, the children, and her mum initially settled in Vienna, about eight hundred kilometres from the western area of Ukraine. By that point, her mum was in desperate need of chemotherapy. 'War started on Thursday, my mum should have had her next chemotherapy on Monday,' she says. They managed to get treatment in Vienna, something that Yuliia is still grateful for. For the following two months, it was just the four of them.

At first they stayed at an apartment in Bratislava – sourced through friends of friends. Then they moved into a one-bedroom place closer to the hospital, to try to ease the pressure on Yuliia. 'I took two small kids in the car, and took my mum [for treatment] every week at 7 a.m.' The three of them keeping themselves busy in the car while her mum had treatment. Yuliia was in a new country, living in a new home, and trying to juggle kids alongside her mum's treatment. It was a lot. That's when Alex made the decision to join them.

But in the interim, Yuliia and her mum tried to make their Vienna accommodation feel more like home. 'When my mum lived with us, preparing food was her responsibility. She liked to prepare food for our kids. It was very special.' Having two adults and two children in such cramped conditions was chaotic and difficult. 'It wasn't possible to make our home feel calm because it was so tiny, and so hard to organise the mess with the kids around.' And then when Alex arrived the situation was made worse. But what did calm them was her mum's cooking.

Yuliia's favourite was when her mum made *tvorog*, a type of cottage cheese which is then used to make *syrnyky* – traditional Ukrainian cheese pancakes, the ingredients of which also include eggs, flour, sugar and salt. But her mum used her skills in the kitchen to prepare other dishes from home, soups like borscht for lunch, small flat dumplings called *varenyky* – fresh dough stuffed full of a variety of fillings, including things like potatoes, mushrooms or meat, but also cherries or blueberries. They sound not dissimilar to the *pierogi* my cousin's Polish mum prepares for me and the kids on occasion. Which are definitely on my list of favourite-ever snacks.

Yuliia's favourite, though, is none of the above. There are two meals she most connects with living at home with her mum. The first is *holubtsi*, which is rolled cabbage leaves stuffed with a mix of rice, meat and vegetables. It's then simmered in a tomato and red pepper sauce. The second is *paska*, traditional Ukrainian Easter bread, which is usually taken to church on Easter morning to be blessed. This was the first Easter that the family had spent together outside of Ukraine, so maintaining that tradition meant a lot to them.

But it was the first Christmas in their current home in London that holds particular significance. It was the final one with Yuliia's mother, and despite only moving in a week before Christmas they were determined to maintain the traditions with which they had been raised. As with most countries in Eastern Europe, it is Christmas Eve, not Christmas Day, that is the main event of the Christmas calendar, and they had a full house: Yuliia's mum, Alex's mum and Alex's grandma, as well as Alex's sister and her family (she moved to London almost twenty years ago).

After ten months of upheaval and uncertainty, the kids were now enrolled in school and pre-school, Alex and Yuliia had found jobs, and Yuliia's mum's treatment had been successful – or so they thought at the time. It felt as though they could finally start preparing the building blocks of stability, and just be still, as well as celebrating them surviving all that had happened to them since February. They threw themselves wholeheartedly into the twelve dishes of *Sviat Vechir* (Ukrainian for Christmas Eve), and the holy supper.

Traditionally, the whole family gathers around one table and eats in the late afternoon once the first star appears in the sky. There are a variety of dishes that can be prepared, but the family's favourite is *kutia* – which is a porridge made from pearl barley with things like honey, jam or dried fruits added to it. But as is true of most traditions, every part of the meal has meaning: the grains symbolise eternal life, and the sweet additions represent heavenly bliss, the dish itself a symbol of unity. There are lots of other traditions included throughout the evening, such as the order in which they are eaten, and children are usually tasked with bringing dinner to the elder members of the family.

'It's important for us to still *feel* Ukrainian, and to keep this feeling. Our children are Ukrainian, and it's important for us to save their language and to keep those traditions in their house, even if they are abroad. Ukrainians made a lot of effort through the ages to keep their identity, through the wars and through genocide,' Yuliia adds.

Their life in London is different to what they are used to, but they are adapting, and the children are thriving at school and pre-school. Yuliia and Alex hope to move somewhere where the kids can once again have a garden to run around in and pick berries, but in the meantime they and the kids have been growing fruits and vegetables in the small, concreted yard they have at the back of their house. It may not be the space they're used to, but they are trying to sprinkle as much of their old life into the second chance that they have been given in the UK. It's interesting when I ask them whether or not they think London will feel like home, because it has echoes of my uncle's feelings towards the UK. 'This country gave us lots of opportunity, so yes I can absolutely call it my *second* home.'

Remember my uncle's reaction to the same question? 'Jamaica is my home, Britain was the land of opportunity.' Although the events that triggered their move to the UK may differ – for my uncle it was to help to rebuild after war, for Alex and Yuliia it was fleeing war – and their stories may be decades apart, their feelings towards the UK are almost exact carbon copies of each other.

No matter where they are in the world, they want to maintain what Yuliia refers to as their Ukrainian 'bubble'. That sentiment is not dissimilar to the story told by another interviewee for this book, Leyli. It's a bubble her father was keen to raise his children in, because both were displaced due to situations that neither of them had any control over, but both scenarios feature the same goal – to make sure their 'home' is not forgotten.

But as to where they now see their home, that's a thought that is ever-changing and developing over time. Yuliia says that she used to refer to home as the place where her and her mum were born, Kosiv, despite being raised in Lviv for most of her life. But the changes that the family has been through over the past eighteen months – both the war and the loss of Yuliia's mum – means that her view is different now. 'I've decided that my home is where my family is, so that it will always be in my heart. So for me, *this* is my new home. I don't want to cry about my previous home. I want to create my new one *here*. Where my family is, where my kids live. I don't know where we will be in a couple of years, but I can take the most important thing from my home – my children – and have a home wherever I am.'

Chapter 5

The Land of No Spice

The list of traditional British foods that I've *not* tasted is not as long as it used to be, but there's still quite a few things that have never really sparked joy for me so I've never really gone out of my way to try them: steak and kidney pie, beef Wellington, Cornish pasty, black pudding, and hotpot are just a few. I have tried haggis, as prepared by a former flatmate, and while I didn't *not* like it, it wasn't something I immediately planned to eat on a regular basis.

This isn't unusual for those of us who've been raised in immigrant households in areas where the population is also crammed full of beautiful cultures living alongside each other, learning from each other and respecting their differences and marvelling at their similarities. The fact that I'd tasted the joy that is Turkish-Cypriot borek before I'd even eaten a Yorkshire pudding is testament to that.

For a number of years, my knowledge of British food didn't really extend beyond fish and chips from the local chippie. In the latter years of primary school and in my early teens my mum started making 'toad in the hole' as a treat ... but that was really the first experience I had of quintessentially British food being prepared at home. We were, like so many immigrant families, a home which had food at its centre. There would always be a container (usually a recycled ice-cream tub) full of leftovers of some capacity in the fridge, which would mean there would always be food at hand should someone pop in unannounced. Culturally, to have a guest leave your home hungry would be seen as hugely disrespectful, and if you dared to offer simply crisps and nuts? You might as well exhibit an act of blasphemy. And people would hear of it, I absolutely promise you they would.

The giving and receiving of food are acts of love. When you have nothing else to give, you feed the bellies of your guests. It doesn't matter if that's a neighbour who's popped in for a chat, or a church sister who's passed by for a cup of tea, or a family celebration. No one must leave your house hungry. And we're not talking a couple of sandwiches and dips, and maybe a cold sausage roll thrown in for good measure – we're talking proper food that takes hours of love, patience and skill to prepare. I'm actually sat here chuckling at the thought of my parents serving up a couple of cheese sandwiches at *any* social occasion in our house; it would just never happen. Not just at our house – it wouldn't happen at *any* social occasion at anybody's house: that's just not how Caribbeans roll. But showing love through the giving of food from your home is a tradition which goes back generations and was born out of survival and necessity.

Historically, my maternal family don't come from very much – they were formerly enslaved and had to rebuild their lives from a patch of land high up in the Clarendon Hills of

Jamaica. But even as enslaved people who were afforded very little from their owners, they would prepare meals not just for themselves, but to ensure the survival of other enslaved people too. The essence of surviving what was a difficult, dark and horrific time in history was to work together as a community, and that community would prepare food together (well, mostly the women would) at 'home' and eat together. This would ensure there was something in the bellies of those who had no choice but to get up every morning and forcibly work for the enrichment of others, the planters. Who, to save the expense of having to feed those they'd enslaved themselves, allocated them tiny bits of land in order to grow their own produce, so the burden of responsibility would be on them to eat enough to survive the hardship that each day brought.

I'm not sure that even 'hardship' accurately describes what it was that they were forced to endure. The explosion of the sugar industry in the eighteenth and nineteenth centuries meant it was big business in the Caribbean, the profits of which would trickle back to line the pockets of the wealthy here in the UK. Who, might I add, were able to go about their day-to-day using the three wise monkey methodology: 'See no evil, hear no evil, speak no evil.' Their hands-off approach absolving them of any responsibility for those being killed *for* them across the Atlantic.

But it wasn't just the middle and upper classes who were enjoying the benefits of the deaths of millions of Black Caribbean people. They were dying at such a rate to cultivate enough sugar to meet demand that those who were deemed working-class could work their way up the class ranks with relative ease through the profits of the sugar trade. So, everyone wanted a piece of the action. Pieces which broke the backs of, and killed, Black Caribbean people at a quicker rate than any other kind of agriculture of the time.

When you see your friends, family and children dying at such a rate around you, I can't possibly imagine what that does to you – especially when those in charge of you view it as a 'normal' side effect of slavery: collateral damage that's worth it. In the shadow of this they not only had to build a home to which they could return their battered and broken bodies every night, but the women had to create foods which they knew could go some way to providing the energy and sustenance required to aid survival. And thus, the creation of what I was raised to call 'hard food' – essentially, foods high in protein and carbohydrates which could, it was hoped, give enslaved people the energy to get up and get going again for another relentless day at the workplace they were forced to attend, never knowing if they'd make it back home alive.

The cultural concept of never letting someone leave your home hungry, and the act of providing proper meals for your community – especially during moments of celebration – was born out of the fundamental need to survive, and of the need to bring some kind of normalcy to a situation which was anything but. These were foods which were, generations later, very much part of the diet I was raised on at home.

We're talking about foods which the generations before my grandparents brought with them when they were forcibly taken from West Africa: okra, yams, breadfruit, ackee plants, plantains, callaloo, mangoes, etc. Meals were then created alongside foods which were indigenous to the area like cassava, plus whatever leftovers the planters would deign to hand over to those they'd enslaved, like salted fish for example. They wouldn't have had much to work with – but out of the few ingredients they had at hand they would create beautifully prepared dishes, which we still eat today.

The routine of what we ate each day came necessarily from a simple structure that my parents could manage at home while working several jobs between them. One of those days would involve 'hard food': boiled potatoes, yams, dumplings, sweet potato, cassava, plantains (and a whole host of other combinations) served with ackee and saltfish. Even writing this list has me salivating at the mere thought of a plate of perfect, well-made ackee and saltfish (a plate that's overcooked just brings a level of disappointment that's unmatched, quite frankly). The ackee must have a little bite, and still be reasonable well formed, and not over-stirred and mushy. A mushy ackee and saltfish is representative of someone in a rush rather than someone softly and patiently stir-frying it with a gentle hand. A rushed and hard hand will cause it to crumble, and over-cooking it causes it to become mushy. A mushy ackee and saltfish is a waste of a beautiful piece of fruit.

If I opened the door after school and could smell a pan of prepared ackee and saltfish, oh, I loved it so. It's not so much the ackee that you could smell but the strong aroma of thyme, onions, Scotch bonnet peppers, a heavy dose of black pepper, a dash of fresh garlic, and of course the saltfish. It's that heady mix of herbs and spices that's the tip-off as to what's been prepared for dinner that night. Growing up, the house filled with the smell of stir-fried salted fish would bring me such joy. But every home's version smells slightly different according to your personalised combination of herbs and spices. And *where* you've purchased your thyme, for example, all makes a difference.

I adore when I rock up at my Aunty Eleanor's house and she's cooked ackee and saltfish for dinner. But hers smells so different to my mum's, and different to mine when I prepare it at home. You could blindfold me and place two bowls of ackee and saltfish in front of me – and from smell alone I could work out which one was my aunt's, and which was my mum's. Both equally as mouth-wateringly gorgeous, but both very different.

The same applied if I had it at grandma's house: she tended to use more peppers than my mum did, and she preferred her ackee softer. Also, the Dutch pot in which it's prepared can cause a slight change in taste – a well-worn and well-oiled Dutch pot produces a very different taste to a recently purchased one. It takes years of meals to own a Dutch pot worthy of producing food that tastes of history and love (the fact that it was my sister that ended up with the family Dutch pot rather than me still enrages me all these years later). One simple fruit can be prepared in exactly the same way, but with slight, almost indistinguishable differences that can completely change the outcome.

Having been born and raised in the UK, I hadn't seen how the ackee fruit grows in its natural state. For me, it had always come out of a can – you open the can, drain the brine then dump it in the pot. I'd not given much thought as to *how* it gets into that can, or how it looked when it wasn't in a can, until a visit to Jamaica in my teens when I watched and helped my Aunty Annette prepare it. It obviously wasn't the first time she'd made it for us, but I was at an age where I was taking more notice of *how* food was prepared when I was there.

She brought out a shopping bag full of tennis ball-sized orange and red circular objects, the tops of which were burst open like a flower, split open into three segments. Each segment was topped by a small black ball – the seed of the fruit. The flesh of each segment is reasonably hard in texture when you break it off, and that's the part that you cook up with your onions and salted fish mix; the black seed and red-orange outer layer you discard. Once you start to cook it up with the mix, the ackee softens as it begins to take on the flavour of the mix and the heat of the oil. And that's the crunch point. You leave it too long and it's a yellow mushy mix with onions and peppers. Leave *just* long enough and it will retain some bite and remain relatively whole. That's the point you're looking for.

When I was growing up, my mum spent a long time in our kitchen teaching me that crunch point. There are particular dishes in Caribbean culture that show the measure of the skills of a cook in a kitchen, and ackee and saltfish is one of them. Its delicate balance of flavours, and the ability to know when it's cooked enough shows a level of understanding about Jamaican cooking. It's a reasonably good indication of someone who's been raised in a Jamaican home. Well, historically, a *woman* who's been raised in a Jamaican home. I know a ton of Jamaican daughters who have impeccable skills in the kitchen – the sons, by comparison, were raised to be tended to (although my dad, after my mum passed, did exceptionally well at producing dishes to perfection).

That well-seasoned side dish is a perfect accompaniment to the blandness that comes from, essentially, a plate of boiled carbs: green bananas, yams, white potatoes, sweet potatoes, etc., which are all boiled to perfection. Which is why salting and oiling the pot of water becomes important because yes, food can look beige and a bit bland, but it absolutely cannot be tasteless.

This dish of seasoned perfection took time to prepare, and my mum would constantly talk me through each step as a kid, so I understood it instinctively. It would start from the night before, soaking the salted fish to release as much of the salt as possible and to soften the meat. We'd then sit together picking out as many of the bones at possible while carefully flaking the flesh. The fish can be delicate too, so overcooking it turns it to mush. Once again, it's all about timing.

Ackee and saltfish would be prepared in abundance in our house, and we'd all hope no one rocked up at the house unannounced that night because otherwise we'd get the leftovers for breakfast, but with slight tweaks. The ackee and saltfish would be reheated, but the circular dreams that were boiled dumplings would be sliced in half and pan-fried on each side, in a method not dissimilar to crumpets, which would caramelise their edges thus creating a crunchier, harder outside and softer inside. If there were *any* dumplings left after breakfast, it would be the biggest miracle known to man. It just never happened.

The other breakfast staple we could only get infrequently was bammy. It's made from cassava, and back then we couldn't get it in the UK – instead, we had to wait for someone to pack large quantities in a suitcase on their visit from

Jamaica. It was a wonderful treat from 'home' that I always looked forward to indulging in. When those flat circular discs of brilliance were pulled out of an aunt's or uncle's suitcase, I'd be itching to get them home to soak in a bowl of milk ahead of being pan-fried the next day.

Interestingly, cassava is one of the few indigenous foods that survived the destruction of the Arawak inhabitants of Jamaica. They are the indigenous community that was 'discovered' by Christopher Columbus when he arrived on the island back in 1494, but which was destroyed by the Spaniards years later. As a concept, the idea that a man can lay claim to an island because he happened to sail there one day and 'discover it' is one of the most dangerous behaviours of Europeans and aided the cultural destruction of so many indigenous communities the world over.

The Arawaks, who are also referred to as the Tainos, arrived from South America thousands of years prior and named the island 'Xaymaca'. They grew cassava, sweet potato, maize, fruits, vegetables, cotton, and tobacco. A list that was clearly a moth to a flame for the Europeans that spent years fighting over who should own it. And in the middle of all this was the native community who, up until that point, had enjoyed a quiet life, before the Europeans waltzed over and saw, not a community that deserved to be left alone, but a community that was getting in the way of mass profits.

But thankfully, the history of so many cultures which have been ripped apart at the seams by various empires can be told through food. When West African enslaved people began to be shipped over to Jamaica, bringing what foods they could from home, it was the few indigenous Arawaks who taught them how to prepare the foods that already existed on the island, like cassava. It's a root vegetable not dissimilar to potatoes or yams. It's like a long, slightly thinner yam, dark brown and tough on the outside, and white on the inside – this is the bit that's edible, but should never be eaten raw; you get to it by peeling the outside with a knife. The ability to use the flesh of the cassava and turn it into cassava flatbread – bammy – is a skill which was passed down from the Arawaks.

Before wheat breads became popular after the Second World War, bammy was the bread staple. The Arawaks taught the West African enslaved people to grate the flesh, place it in a woven bag, leave it outside in a press to get rid of much of the moisture, beat it in a mortar and then sieve to a flour-like consistency. This cassava flour is what's used to make the bammy flatbread, a rich and affordable source of carbohydrates, high in calories. Essential for a day spent out in the fields, but way too labour-intensive to make from scratch in a kitchen in south-east London – as if any member of my family would have the time or patience to do all of the above, even if they could find a good piece of cassava.

Instead, the bread itself was sent over from Jamaica pre-prepared; you then cut it into triangles and rehydrate it by soaking in cows' milk or coconut milk before pan-frying it. The result is something that has the sturdiness of a McDonald's hash brown, I guess, with a crunch as you bite into it, but a softness that's slightly harder than potatoes. It can be served with just about anything, but I love it on its own, dipped in a dollop of ketchup.

The food that helped aid the survival of those enslaved people who were able to last the average twenty years of life during servitude has remained virtually unchanged over the centuries: in terms of its preparation, the way in which it is served, and the importance that's placed on it within the family home. How incredible is that? The planters, slave-masters, and those who benefitted financially here in the UK took virtually *everything* else: their children, their bodies, their independence, wages, and most importantly, their lives. The one thing they *could* pass on, was the thing they desperately needed in order to survive what they were forced to go through: food. The thing that became central in their homes (if you could call them that) remained central in the homes of the generations that followed. It was, incredibly, the one thing that could *not* be taken away, because to those that owned enslaved people, most of their 'native food' had no monetary value to them, so was therefore of little to no importance to them: the sole reason it survived. This meant that generation after generation of Jamaican homes, both on the island and further afield, could keep those traditions.

If you hail from somewhere else in the world, there tends to be a very present need to ensure that your home reflects where you're from and that your children – though born in the UK – have an understanding of their roots. Hence why, as I've mentioned previously, I always think of my home growing up as being a slice of Jamaica in a little corner of London.

I'll caveat that with saying that, yes, the need of my parents and grandparents to carve out that space came from pride in where they were from, but also because there weren't many other options at hand. Assimilating themselves into British culture was nigh-on impossible; they weren't exactly welcomed with open arms. Instead, the strength and power came from sticking with what they knew. But also, why *should* they give up all they knew and forget where they were from? For a start, they were invited to Britain to help rebuild it, and unlike when the British Empire forced British values onto communities the world over, immigrants were, and still are, merely trying to live alongside the British with a mixture of both. The hypocrisy tends to be lost.

Despite the irrational pushback, one of the beautiful things about Britain – and one that should be relentlessly celebrated – is the aforementioned melting pot of cultures that live on this little island. It's a superpower that we don't shout from the rooftop nearly enough.

As of the end of 2022, 14.8% of the UK population were not born in the UK,[1] but that figure masks the likes of me who were raised in immigrant communities in the UK, a figure which is far higher. According to ONS figures, during 2022 the percentage of births where either one or both parents were born outside the UK was 36.7% in England, and 16.1% in Wales[2] – again, a figure which reflects the huge range of cultures and traditions that can be added to Britain's tally. For a country which changed and destroyed so much of the world's cultures and traditions, it really is something to see how, over time, so many cultures can now call it home.

Leyli's experiences of being the child of immigrants mirrored so much of the way I grew up (I'm not including her surname, so it's safer for her and her family). Her experience, though, isn't from a Caribbean perspective – her father is originally from Iran, her mother Irish Catholic, and the family settled in Cardiff in Wales. 'Mine is a large, culturally diverse family,' she says. 'I grew up in a chaotic household with a lot of love.' That chaotic household also involved making sure that whoever crossed the threshold into their home was always fed, so that they would leave happy. 'Iranian culture is the most hospitable culture. No one is allowed to leave the house hungry, and they don't take no for an answer.' She explains that tradition states that a guest has to say no three separate times before the host finally stands down and stops offering. The three-strike rule doesn't exist in Jamaica – refusing to eat food which has been prepared is just plain rude and won't go down well. So they'll just keep on offering until you relent.

When Leyli talks about the home she grew up in in Wales, it just sounds so colourful, so hectic, so, yes, full of love as she describes it. There are some homes where you know their inhabitants plodded along with a level of calm and subdued excitement; I definitely imagine Leyli's house to be the opposite, with family popping in and out routinely, and quiet moments few and far between. The path that she took in her adult life was sparked by her experiences of being raised in a home full of culture and tradition. Just like my parents passed on the skills needed to successfully and authentically prepare food from where they came from, so too did Leyli's mum and dad. But the focus on attention to detail that her dad implemented with Leyli was definitely a level above my parents, which would explain why she's now a chef and I'm a broadcaster.

Much like me, Leyli grew up in a family with cousins who all live relatively close to each other. 'Because of my mum's Irish Catholic family I've got hundreds of cousins.' Her generation has at least twenty cousins all born within the same timeframe. The joy with which she talks about her home is infectious. 'Food has always been at the centre,' she says. There were no small meals, only big ones involving the whole family – including her three siblings – and whoever else was around that day, gathered round the table indulging in the smells and tastes of Iran. Although from an Irish Catholic background, her mum threw herself wholeheartedly into the Iranian culture her husband was raised in and was taught by her mother-in-law how to prepare the food he had been raised with, before the move to the UK.

The reasons why Leyli's dad ended up in the UK are vastly different from how my parents ended up here. He had already left the country by the time Iran's 1979 revolution kicked in, with three of the brothers following suit setting up home elsewhere in the world: Tokyo, Toronto and LA. One brother chose to stay in Tehran. Still close despite the distance, the repercussions of the revolution are still felt throughout the family, with a generation who feel a huge connection to, and are protective of, a country they've never been able to visit.

The Iranian Revolution – carried out to 'defend the oppressed' and to restructure Iran and other societies in the Islamic World – ended with the Pahlavi dynasty being overthrown in 1979, and the monarch Mohammed Reza Shah being ousted. In the decades before the Islamic Revolution the Shah's dictatorship repressed dissent and restricted political freedoms; however, he was a believer in Western-orientated secular modernisation – including social, political and economic change which allowed for a level of cultural freedom. It was called the White Revolution. But many were distrustful of the cultural influence of the West and the new elite class that was emerging in Iran; some felt that Iranians were getting high on the thought of aligning themselves with the West and pushing back against the building blocks from which the country was built.

During this time women's rights improved – they were encouraged to get an education and were allowed to mix with men, they gained the right to vote in the mid-1960s and were elected to parliament. Iran's economy expanded, with both Britain and the US counting Iran as an ally. But despite the cultural freedoms, it was the Shah's insistence on no dissent – like ordering police to forcibly remove headscarves for example – and getting rid of multi-party rule that helped set the stage for the revolution. So too did the fear of Western influence on society as a whole. For many, the belief was that a return to a more authentic and Islamic identity would be the remedy.[3,4]

In its place came Islamic theocracy, which, among other things, rolled back seventy years of advancement of women's rights – included things like forcing women to wear the headscarf. A return to a life unrecognisable to the one Iranians had been living for the past forty years prompted the largest number of people at one time leaving the country to find homes elsewhere.

Those fleeing to study abroad were the first wave to leave in the years leading up to, and including the revolution, as well as families closely associated with the monarchy, and those who were part of religious minorities. The second phase – post-revolution – involved the more liberal elements of the population: young men who didn't want to serve in the Iran-Iraq War, and young families – especially those with daughters.

They didn't feel able, or want to, live under the constraints – as they saw it – of Islamic rule: very little education, forced to wear a veil, and being forced to obey the men in the family.[5]

Leyli's father, however, had long left Iran by the time the revolution kicked in in 1979. He'd moved to the UK many years beforehand at the age of fifteen. A lack of English meant that he spelt his family name slightly wrong on arrival. The miscommunication means that Leyli shares a different surname to the rest of the Iranian side of her family, a quirk which is not unusual for those who have arrived from elsewhere. In fact, there has constantly been discussion in my own maternal family about the correct spelling of their surname. No one really knew the correct one. It was only through going back into official records that we realised that the confusion had happened via slave records, which showed a phonetical spelling of the surname, rather than the official one. And over the years the family had been using both.

Much like so many immigrants who move to the UK from far-flung warmer climates, the thing that sticks out about the country other than the unpredictable weather is the lack of spices used in its foods. Although imperialism and colonialism introduced the UK to more than just a pinch of salt and some mustard, that didn't always translate to the foods that we perceive as quintessentially British. Salt can give a *little* flavour, but using *just* salt? No, it's just not right. I remember my mum in fits of laughter watching cooking shows on the TV at home when chefs would neither wash their chicken, nor season it sufficiently. The effect was *obviously* tasteless chicken, and yet this was held in higher esteem than chucking in any kind of flavour.

I think it's this view of British food that mostly put my parents off British cooking initially. They had been raised on a diet packed full of spices, herbs and flavour, on an island that was famed for its variety of tastes, and a beautiful array of colourful dishes. So too was Leyli's dad: Persian food is known for its delicate embrace of flavours that's at odds with the strong and spicy nature of Jamaican fare. But nonetheless, both were the antithesis of what is considered traditional British food. And back in the 1970s, the availability of spices to successfully recreate the dishes which Leyli's dad had grown up with was sparse. So as a young man who no doubt missed home, the boiled ham and potatoes that was made available to him by his landlady was just not going to cut it.

He eventually found himself in a situation whereby if he was going to make Cardiff feel like home, he would have to learn to cook himself. 'He'd never even eaten ham before, so he became such a good cook because he had to learn to cook for himself because he wouldn't eat anyone else's food.' I can just imagine how a young man who'd grown up with food that was so full of colour, and so packed full of variety, viewed that which was on offer in the UK.

Due to him being self-taught, he became fussy with not only how *he* prepared his food, but how those skills were taught to Leyli and her siblings. 'He was harsh when I'd be cooking at home. He would be like, "No, cut that tomato thinner." He was so particular. I got used to perfecting things at such a young age without realising.' Unlike me, Leyli can't return to the country of her father's birth to observe and surround herself with the foods and cooking traditions that she grew up hearing her dad talk about with such love, respect and passion – which will be why teaching her and her siblings what he knew became so much more important.

Without that link to the past, the fear was that the culture which had been such a big part of the person he had become would be lost for ever. Home is intrinsically linked to how we feel about ourselves, and how we view ourselves. Her father didn't want that to be lost in a family that wasn't able to see it for themselves in Iran, so he worked hard to recreate that at home. This means that despite not being raised in Iran, Leyli is incredibly patriotic about the country. 'It's funny, even though I wasn't brought up there, there's something ingrained in me. I feel this huge sense of belonging.'

Her dad met her mum in a wine bar in Cardiff on a night out in the early 1970s. Her mum, with her Michelle Pfeiffer looks and big personality, was spotted by her dad instantly across the room. But it took a whole year for him to pluck up the courage to ask her out. This coming together of cultures, Irish and Iranian, though beautiful, caused issues for the young couple. They had, as Leyli describes it, 'a fight on their hands'. In the village-like environment that was Cardiff back then, they had to prove that they deserved to be with each other, with Leyli's mum losing hairdressing clients because they were so repulsed by the choices she had made by marrying a foreigner.

Meeting so long before the revolution meant that he could safely show her the country that had his heart, and walk her through the streets he'd been raised in. It meant that both Leyli's mum and dad could extol the virtues and the beauty of this far-flung country. Leyli and her siblings could only learn from her parents' memories, and pictures. But everything came with such heart, and such love, the children's connection to it became undeniable, and over the years just grew ever-stronger.

'It's talked about every day in our home. A lot changed in Iran, and we were brought up with a lot of the old stories before the revolution. My mum went before the revolution, so she saw the good and great times that they were having before it all turned upside down.' The country her dad knew no longer exists, and so she says that's probably why they've been brought up on stories about how great it was, 'because it *was* great'.

Much like you often only remember the good bits of a person once they're dead and gone, I guess the same applies when it comes to losing a country. Only the good remains in the memory bank, and they are the stories that her dad wants to share. Both he and Leyli's mum wanted them to feel as proud of Iran pre-revolution as they did. 'Yes,' she says, 'that hits the nail on the head. There are so many stories brought up with a history of a very proud family.'

She would hear tales of her dad's uncle who was the doctor of the Shah of Iran (Mohammed Reza Pahlavi), and her dad's aunt, who was a lady-in-waiting to the Ashraf Pahlavi – the Shah's twin sister. She was widely seen as the power behind her brother, and instrumental in the coup which put her brother on the throne back in 1953. She was also a staunch supporter of women's rights, and was exiled after the revolution. An assassination attempt in France in 1977 saw multiple bullets fired into the side of her car, but although Ashraf survived, Leyli's great-aunt was killed.

You can understand the pride Leyli's father had for his family and the country of his birth, and why he doesn't want those memories to be lost. For if he doesn't share them, the fear, of course, is that those first-hand memories will disappear for ever, left to be retold only in books and in pictures, not passed down through the generations where the memories hold the most weight.

These are the stories that regaled Leyli and her siblings multiple times, from a father that was proud of his family and his heritage, and who wanted to recreate the home he had had in Iran, in South Wales. A lot of this will be tied to the fact it's not safe for Leyli and her siblings to travel to Iran, as set out in the rules from the Foreign Office who have advised British travellers against all travel. But her father does on occasion return to see the handful of family he has left there. Although when he goes it's a reminder, yet again, of what he feels his country has lost, and what it no longer represents. 'It's really sad when my dad goes back now,' Leyli says. 'Every time he comes back, he says he'll never [return again]. But he does.'

The pull of the country of his birth, she says, is still so strong, despite the changes which are so at odds with the version of the country that sits in his heart. That country has gone, disappeared virtually overnight. In its place, a constitution and a regime that is far more oppressive than the one that was overthrown all those years ago: the authoritarian regime replaced with a religious authoritarianism. The class divides replaced by *new* class divides: the gap between the poor and middle classes, and the moneyed upper classes as gaping as it was pre-revolution.

Leyli's mum being able to experience the 'before' appears key to the love the whole household has for her father's home. In her mum he found someone that would grow to love that heritage. 'Mum was obsessed with Persian food, with Iranian food. She was taught by my paternal grandmother. She had no background in cooking or anything, just good solid techniques of cooking from *her* mum. But when she met my dad she was introduced to this whole new world, and she totally absorbed it.' The pride that she has for her mum is so evident: 'She took things into her own interpretation, she would tweak things. And she was good at it.'

Sunday lunch for Leyli, much like in my home growing up, didn't resemble the Sunday roast that Britain is famed for. And it sounds glorious. 'We would have a barbecue, that was our traditional Sunday lunch,' taking on the traditional gender roles in the cooking process. Her dad would man the barbecue, her mum in charge of the rest of the meal. She laughs: 'It's funny because that's the role I've gone into. So when we're preparing food it doesn't matter that I'm a classic-ally trained chef; I've got all this experience when it comes to the family barbecue. I'm relegated to sides.'

It is her mum who's in charge of the main event, the centrepiece of the table: the *Tahdig*. It's a rice dish that she describes as being 'basically a rice cake'. It's not the type of rice cake that you may be thinking of, which for most of us is the familiar snacking variety. No, it's a *cake* made of rice that is painstakingly delicate to make and involves all matter of stages that can vary according to your family or local trad-ition. 'There's a big celebration when you turn the rice out of the pot and reveal it at the table.'

In so many cultures, the meats are the main part of a meal, with rice, vegetables and potatoes acting as sides to accompany the main event that has taken hours to prepare.

But in Iranian tradition, that is switched on its head. The meat becomes the side, and the rice is the jewel in the crown. Hence the crowd-pleasing 'big reveal' at the end. Leyli calls it 'extremely simple', and yet when she talks me through it, it doesn't *quite* sound like something a novice would refer to as such.

It involves parboiling the rice until it's al dente, passing it through a sieve to drain off the water, then cooling it down so that the grains grow longer. You then melt a lot of butter in a non-stick pan. In some recipes you can add yoghurt, potatoes, saffron, even some flatbread. You put the rice into the pan then cook gently for at least an hour. When you turn it out, it has produced a beautiful crust, 'so it's super soft and fluffy on the inside, but you crack open the golden crust and everyone fights over that part'. She explains that it's not dissimilar to the tasty crusty bits you get on a lasagne or paella. 'There are hundreds of different ways to do it.'

Although rice isn't the main event of a Jamaican meal, it certainly features heavily in various forms. There are myriad ways to prepare rice that extend beyond the traditional rice and peas: callaloo rice, vegetable rice, prawn rice to name a few. But if you steam the rice for a smidge too long and it caramelises at the bottom of the pot, kids can often be found picking at the bottom of the pot to munch on the crusty bits. I realise that rather than throw away such a clearly adored part of the dish, they've made it the main draw. Which is quite genius, really.

Despite being the main event of a meal, *Tahdig* isn't the meal that most connects her to home – it's her mum's saffron chicken. 'It's her twist on a Persian dish, it's her interpretation of it. And it's delicious.' She talks me through the process, and by the end I am pleading with her to put a date in the diary so I could go round to her parents for dinner, and have her mum cook enough for me to pack some up and take back to London.

'It's chicken that's braised with orange, saffron, butter and barberries [small dried sweet and sour berries], which act almost as a sweetener.' The dish is served with her mum's jewelled rice: 'The "jewels" come from the different kinds of dried fruits and nuts or varying colours to represent gems.' There are hundreds of recipes with different variations of rice, so again it's something that's individual to every family. 'It's unique, and not something you'll find in an Iranian restaurant. It's my mum's interpretation of the dish. And that, for me, that's home.'

She's absolutely right, you know – one of the dishes I most associate my mum with isn't a dish that most people would link to Jamaica. It's an interpretation of a dish which originated back in the nineteenth century when Chinese immigrants arrived in Jamaica to also work on plantations (with a second wave arriving in the early 1900s). They brought with them different ingredients and different ways of cooking: rice is a prime example, but so too are noodles. Neither was a staple until Chinese immigrants arrived, and yet rice and peas are now very common, as is a Jamaican take on chow mein. My most-loved dish from my mum is along the lines of chow mein, and it didn't matter how many times I tried recreating it when she was alive or after she passed, I can never quite make it taste the same.

We'd have it about once a month on a Tuesday. How on Earth do I know that, I hear you ask. Well, as I've mentioned previously, we had certain meals on certain days to make life easier for my full-time working parents: on a Sunday it would be a traditional Caribbean Sunday dinner, and on Monday would be the leftovers. Sometimes the Monday meal would involve using the leftover rice and peas for egg fried rice, with the addition of frozen peas and a dash of soy sauce (another classic). This would leave the chicken leftover for a Tuesday meal, which would be crispy chow mein noodles – a meal that is basically as it describes. It would be slightly more time-consuming because you had to fry the egg noodles in batches after you'd cooked them per the instructions on the packet. Then you'd add them to the stir-fried mixture of garlic, ginger, onions, sweet peppers, and the leftover chicken. If I knew I was getting that on a Tuesday after school, I was genuinely so excited. It felt posh.

In a similar way that Leyli's mum's dish is an interpretation of a classic Iranian dish, my mum's crispy chow mein was her interpretation of a Chinese-Jamaican dish. It's the recipe of hers that I find most difficult to recreate in *exactly* the same way. And it's the meal I miss the most. I wish I'd spent more hours having her teach me. But hindsight is a wonderful thing, right?

The 'exotic' nature of the food in Leyli's house made her popular among her friends in South Wales. They were brought up on a diet of traditional English and Welsh food, so walking through the door of her family home would mean a meal so different to what they were used to. 'I had friends whose parents didn't cook, and I was like, "What do you eat?!"' And with the explosion of frozen food in the '80s and '90s, it meant that she was introduced to food that wasn't freshly prepared when she went to friend's houses for tea after school. But she definitely preferred her parents' freshly cooked meals, which became popular among her mates, thus ensuring that the Iranian traditions in their home stretched further than their front door. This in turn gave Leyli's friends a greater understanding of the traditions and cultures of this far-away land.

The impact of Leyli's home on others was solidified when her best friend, who's British, got married, and her choice of main meal for the wedding reception was Iran's national dish, *ghormeh sabzi*, cooked by Leyli. A meal that reminded *her* of her childhood. How incredible is that? 'I think it was probably my proudest moment,' she says, explaining how much it meant to her, how people saw her so connected to her Iranian background and home, and how much her friends were connected to it too. 'It's slow braised lamb with fenugreek, omani limes, and a ton of herbs. It's really light and really aromatic.'

It's also the dish that Iranians have at *Nowruz*, which is the Persian New Year, a celebration which her friends had witnessed countless times over the years in Leyli's home. *Nowruz* means 'new day' and marks both the arrival of spring and the first day of the year in Iran, whose solar calendar begins with the vernal equinox. It's an event which has been celebrated in Iran and the Persian diaspora for more than three thousand years. The celebration has roots as a feast day in Zoroastrianism, one of the world's oldest faiths thought to go back to the second millennium BCE. It centres on the arrival of spring, which is seen as a victory over darkness. It's a celebration that clearly means a lot for the culture since it survived not only the Islamic conquest of

Persia in the seventh century, but also the fall in popularity of Zoroastrianism.[6]

The majority of Jamaica follows the Christian faith, but also has pockets of Judaism, Hinduism, Buddhism, Islam and Rastafarianism – a reflection of the beauty within its mix of cultures. As previously mentioned, my family are Christian, so the traditions in my home tended to align with the British calendar events such as Easter and Christmas. Fun fact: Jamaica holds the Guinness World Record for the most churches per square mile, something which becomes fairly obvious as you drive around the island. You can't go far without spotting another. Christianity was brought by the Spanish in the sixteenth century, therefore its roots aren't as long embedded in Jamaica as Zoroastrianism. So listening to Leyli's stories of the way in which Persian New Year was celebrated in her home is fascinating.

It happens on the first day of spring, so the date changes every year ... but there's two weeks of build-up to the big day. Leyli compares it to the build-up of the week before Christmas straight through to New Year's Day. She says every day is a celebration in the lead-up, including friends and family coming round for dinner. Her home would be full for days.

As a part of the build-up, they have a Haft-Seen table: 'Haft' is Persian for seven, and 'Seen' is the fifteenth letter of the Persian alphabet. On the table, as Leyli describes it, are seven items which start with the letter 'S'. That includes *Sumac*, which is a symbol of contentment, *Sib* (apple), which represents health, and *Senjed* (Sea-buckthorn), which is regarded as a symbol of wisdom. It also includes a goldfish, which, although it obviously *doesn't* start with the letter 'S', is considered as one of the elements of *Nowruz* in Iran, because its vibrant red colour symbolises kindness, victory, livelihood and affluence.

It is, though, the growing of *Sabzeh*, lentil sprouts, which Leyli most enjoys. It represents life: new life, renewal, rebirth and celebration. Her mum would take charge of growing the *Sabzeh* from a type of lentil. On the final day of *Nowruz*, the grass which has been grown from the dry seeds would be simply thrown away: 'You go to a river and discard it,' Leyli explains. 'And that's the way of casting out the evil eye, or any bad feelings so that you are protected.' It's part of a flurry of superstitions that she's taken on board from her Iranian side. It's not that she necessarily believes in it, but if she *didn't* do it, she says that she would end up feeling something akin to Catholic guilt. So the family sticks to the traditions, just in case.

There is, though, one part of his heritage that Leyli's father didn't fully share with his children in their home, and as a result Leyli does feel a slight detachment from the culture so embraced by her father: Farsi. Her dad never taught it to them, despite being bilingual himself. Traditionally it's believed that Farsi is a mother's tongue, therefore it's the mother's job to teach, so her dad didn't feel the need to teach them himself. 'I'm quite angry that he didn't enforce it, nor enforce it on us, or really encourage us to learn. I would have loved to be able to speak it.' She can, however, understand some of it if she hears it. She feels the same about not knowing how to speak Welsh, having been raised in South Wales. Not being able to speak either language leaves her in limbo a bit.

Although Jamaica's official language is English, they also

speak Patois, a Creole dialect which has been created from Jamaica's colonial heritage, with influences from the West African language Akan, along with Spanish, Irish, Chinese, German and many more. It's a dialect that I was around daily, but although I understand it, I don't speak it fluently. Several members of my family lost their heavily accented Patois when they moved to the UK, tired of the obstacles and hoops they had to jump through to progress in life – so over time their accents and dialects softened. As was the case with my mum and my aunt, some accents drifted away for ever.

Having lived briefly in Thailand and London, Leyli understands what it is to be out of that gorgeous home environment. But each time she was away trying out new things and sampling different ways of life, the pull of her old life, the one that knows and loves – the one among her family – was too much to completely let go of. And I can absolutely understand that. Much like her father constantly feels the pull to the home in which he was raised, she too feels the draw to the beautiful Iranian/Irish/Welsh collage that is her life in her home town. As cool as somewhere like London was to live, it was never going to be home for her. But it's not the physical home that is the place that she would say she feels more at home. She talks very little about the physical aspects of the house that she grew up in in South Wales, its surroundings, or the local area. These aspects are secondary to what connects her to her home. Home for her is centred on the people and traditions in her house, and the cosy feel of the security blanket which is having extended family just a walk away.

For Leyli the idea of home centres around wherever her

family and friends are. 'It's not a specific place, and it's not specifically Wales. It's when I'm around my family, and I equally feel at home when I'm around my friends.' She then throws in a line that even she finds cheesy: 'Home is where the heart is,' she laughs.

Which, I guess, is the point of why her dad raised his children in the way he did. The revolution meant that his heart could never fully return to Iran, no matter how much he may have wanted to. The country it became was not the country he left, and no amount of hope could change that. So he created a replica Iran of sorts in Wales, to placate the grief he obviously felt at losing the home that he loved dearly.

Despite his heart being broken at the loss of his country, he mended it the only way he could. By showing the love he had for his country to his children, the hope was that they would fall in love with it too. And it worked, but what he also created within them was not anchoring their hearts to a particular place or particular building – instead, they tied them to family.

Home for Leyli 'means family, and food. It's the centre. When I think of that, I naturally think of being sat around the dinner table. That's always been our centre.'

Chapter 6

Serving Your Country

I come from a forces family: my dad was in the RAF and my Uncle Errol was in the Army. The only memory I have of my dad's RAF past is his huge military coat – called a greatcoat – that used to cover the water tank in our airing cupboard. I used to see every time I went to grab a towel, or pack the towels away, and it became like a piece of the furniture that I didn't really notice after a while. But one day I finally decided to ask *why* there was a random coat hanging in the cupboard, and it was then that my dad told me it was from his days in the RAF. Unfortunately, there aren't any pictures of my dad in full uniform, but I imagine him looking handsome and quite grand and important, with him wearing the uniform rather than the uniform wearing him. He's a tall man, my dad, and he would have looked fabulous.

My uncle's stint in the Army was far longer; he was stationed in Germany during my younger years. He's proud, as he should be, of his time in the British Army. And no matter where he's lived there is always a picture of him in full uniform in his living room. He too was a man who could *really* pull off a military uniform; it's fairly obvious why he was popular with ladies back then (a phenomenon that exists to this day).

My dad joined the RAF young, aged just seventeen-and-a-half, a year after he arrived in the UK from Jamaica. He says it wasn't a difficult decision for him to go, because things were so difficult at home. He was the final child to be 'sent for' by his parents. The routine back then for Jamaican immigrants to the UK was that the parents would make the journey first, either together or individually, then would be joined by each child – usually one by one – as and when they could afford it. My paternal grandad arrived first in 1955, followed by my grandma and my Aunty Cynthia. My dad, meanwhile, was sent to live with his uncle, at just four years old. He wasn't sent for until 1967, twelve years after his father first made that journey. In the intervening years, his three additional sisters were born in the UK.

My dad was part of what's now known as 'barrel children', the children abandoned or 'left behind' by their parents who were looking for a better life somewhere else – usually America or Britain. This extreme level of parent-child separation brought a level of emotional trauma, the trickle effect of which can still be felt within Caribbean families even today. The term was created by Dr Claudette Crawford-Brown, and although the term is unique to Jamaica, the phenomenon is not.

Children and their parents being separated due to migration is something that occurs regularly, even today. The research into the psychological impact on children has been studied multiple times over the decades. Most notably, the research shows that these children were often raised by surrogate parents who *did* love them but were unable to give them the emotional support they needed as a consequence of having their parents up and leave (in my dad's case, for over a decade). The emotional scars can take generations to heal, if they heal at all. The list of behavioural changes as a result of having to grieve for parents who aren't actually dead include depression, and withdrawal. Which, in the circumstances, is completely understandable.

In the Caribbean, and especially Jamaica, you essentially have a whole generation of kids whose 'home' was taken away, not by faceless strangers in search of power, but by the ones who loved them. The economics of the situation meant it was the best way to financially move an entire family to a different continent, but the frequent consequence was the creation of hairline fractures which became larger and larger over time, in some cases causing irreparable breaks in parental relationships.

This is what my dad was dealing with emotionally when he made the journey from the home he knew to the new one, and a family which had essentially abandoned him. True, he was left behind because they couldn't afford to take him at that time, and yet in the intervening years before they finally allowed him to join them, they had had more children. Emotionally, the move for my dad in 1967 was hard. He was suddenly faced with a very different family dynamic than the one that had walked away from him in Jamaica. I can't even begin to fathom how a sixteen-year-old is meant to successfully deal with that, or how it was expected that he would just slot in and everything would be fine. As if the previous twelve years hadn't happened. Calling the adjustment 'hard' doesn't even begin to scratch the surface.

This teenager, on the cusp of adulthood, was having to work out how he felt about the parents who had left him for so long to be raised by his uncle, while at the same time figure out his new home of London, while *also* figuring out how he fit into this new family dynamic *and* his new British-born sisters. Every time my dad tells me the story, my heart just feels so much love and devastation for the little boy that was thrown into an impossible situation.

It comes as no surprise that home life was difficult for my dad. He felt like he just didn't fit, no matter how hard he tried. We have more of an understanding about trauma now, and my dad was clearly going through a lot of trauma that was never dealt with. I can imagine that back then, the idea of repairing your relationship with your child just wasn't a thing. It was more of a sink-or-swim situation: 'Things were hard at home with mummy, so I left,' he tells me. He joined the RAF. Like so many young people, the draw to the military for him was a chance to get away, so he signed up for five years. He lasted just a year living with his family, but this time it was *his* choice to leave, not a decision that was foisted upon him.

Initial training was in Lincolnshire for six weeks, and then he was posted to St Athan in South Wales. In Jamaica he had been part of the Jamaican Combined Cadet Force, so he was already aware of what military life was like and it didn't come as a shock. He had various postings over the years and made lifelong friends – including one of his best friends, my Uncle Norman. His final posting was at Brize Norton in Oxfordshire, and once this came to an end, he was ready to leave. But in those five years he was able to learn more about who he was outside of that fractured family environment, and probably heal to be honest. It would have given him a chance to figure out what he wanted to make of his new home in England. He missed elements of his Jamaican life, though, especially the food, so weekend visits back to the family home came with the advantages of home-cooked food.

He got a lot out of creating a home in the RAF, including structure, discipline, and a good work ethic. All things that were instrumental in terms of the father that he went on to become. Choosing to sign up probably saved my dad, to be honest, and it showed quite a high level of wherewithal for someone so young to take that path rather than one which could have had a very different and unpleasant ending. As a result, he will always be proud of the opportunity that it gave him. It meant that when he left the RAF five years later, he was emotionally stronger and able to cultivate a home for himself in the UK, meet my mum, and create his own family. On his own terms.

For James (not his real name) though, choosing to join the military came from a very different perspective, although there was crossover with my dad's story as James was also in the Combined Cadet Force while at school in the UK. The seed that took him into the skies for the Navy was sown early on. But his love for travel, and not really setting down proper roots, goes back far further.

As a young child aged just two, his family moved to Malawi from the UK for his father's job. His first memories are growing up in what sounds like the most incredible compound. He lived there until he was eight, cycling around the compound and hanging out around the pool playing with his friends. The family also had a small place in Nkhotakota, which is a port town in Central Malawi on the shores of Lake Malawi. 'I've got memories of going there and sleeping there, swimming in the lake every day and getting eaten alive by various bugs,' he says.

It sounds like the most beautiful home to grow up in for someone so young. But the compound was quintessentially British, so it was more like a home away from home, with the addition of cleaners, cooks, nannies and whatever else the British workers and their families needed to make the experience easier. It was more of a colonial-esque upbringing which was, he realises as an adult, an environment which allowed for a certain level of privilege.

During the family's time there, his parents split up. James and his brother ended up on a plane with his mum, heading to a new place that he could call home, in Rutland in the East Midlands: 'I remember not wanting to leave, and I remember my brother and I hiding under one of the airplane blankets at one point, crying.' Flying away from the only home he'd ever known at that point left him devastated, but it meant that he was moving closer to family, and the advantage of being a child so young was that his recovery was swift. 'I think as a child, you probably just accept what's put in front of you a lot of the time, and just think, "Okay, this is probably normal."'

But his connection to Malawi never waned, with moments of nostalgia over the years as he remembered more snippets of his time there, meaning that there's a level of familiarity and warmth when he talks about the country. It was such a unique experience to have, it would be hard not to assume that the years spent there had an impact on the way he viewed the world, and it's a part of his identity, he says. 'I feel an emotional pull to Malawi; it was such a large part of my life. It was an amazing adventure.'

The joy he gleaned from being outdoors features a lot in the story of what home means to James. The family's new home in the East Midlands had a large garden which has left him with memories of running around it all the time with his brother, and spending most of their time outside. 'The outdoors was always quite a big element of our upbringing.' Living abroad for so long sparked a love for 'being elsewhere', he says. After university he spent a gap year travelling around Africa, and has subsequently done a lot travelling outside of the military, because of a yearning he feels for learning about the world and experiencing more of it.

By this point the family dynamic had changed, and his home in Rutland altered slightly when his mum, having met someone new years earlier, settled down with her partner. He and his brother officially gained step-siblings. His natural next step after university was to go into banking, as that's what several of his uni mates were doing, but a conversation one night with his step-brother Rob – who was in the Army at the time – changed the course of his life. He and his step-brother had known each other for years by this point and Rob questioned if he'd ever thought more about the love of flying that he'd had since being a teenager. Off the back of that conversation, Rob suggested that James look into joining the Navy as a pilot.

He was on the move again. James and I have lived very different lives. Until I was twenty-five I'd only ever lived in two homes, both with my parents and siblings. I hadn't experienced long periods of living elsewhere, which is probably why

I have such a draw towards my family home. But it's slightly different for James, I think. By the time he left to join the Navy, he'd had multiple homes and schools in different countries, then university, then travelling. Calling him a nomad is probably quite extreme, but it's not far off. Although he feels a pull to Malawi, it's not one that would see him up sticks to move back, and even though he has the most wonderful memories of his mother's house, the emotional connection there feels different.

As a result, when he left to join the Navy there were no feelings of homesickness. The initial officer training was in Dartmouth, at the Britannia Royal Naval College. There he learnt how to be in the military. It was all marching, taking orders, jumping, running around, putting on kit and running around on Bodmin Moor: 'Sleeping outside, getting cold, getting wet and all that stuff.' He clearly loved it, although to me it sounds horrendous! The next stage was on a ship, with ten weeks of learning about life at sea. They had shared dorms of differing sizes housing twelve to sixteen men at a time (although there was a bigger one, nicknamed 'the zoo', which housed thirty or more).

My guess is that it wasn't homely, since it literally sounds the direct opposite of that. 'No it wasn't,' he laughs, 'but that was part of the fun. I've still got fond memories.' He credits his brief boarding-school experience with giving him the tools to cope with it, especially since, he says, the likes of the Dartmouth training centre initially started out as boarding schools. Which goes some way to explain why some thrive in that environment, and others don't.

Most importantly though, he didn't miss home. All his

time spent outside of his mum's house and being away from his dad meant that being apart from them both was his normal, and when he did have a short period at home after university, it just made him desperate to leave. 'I think I was sick of being at home, and was more than ready to leave again. So that saved me from *any* feelings of homesickness.'

The preference to living at home? Living on a ship with eight hundred people. Eight. Hundred. People. In an environment, a home, where you barely even see any daylight. That is quite something for the mind to deal with. 'Unlike a cruise ship where you'll have a window or a porthole or whatever you want to call it, you're in a mess together.' And the nature of the job meant you rarely spoke to anybody *not* on the ship.

It's a home environment I think I would struggle in; I'm just not wired in the same way as James, and it's genuinely fascinating to hear him speak about it. He lived in a room that housed thirty men in what he calls 'gulches'. He explains: 'You walk through the door and have loads of rows going off, and that was the gulch. You might have three beds long and three beds high. So you'd have nine beds on each side, then you'd have another gulch.' (I looked it up and a gulch is an area of the mess deck between the bunks.) He then goes on to explain what other space there was on the ship – a communal recreation space with a TV and a small amount of soft seating, and some small lockers to put your stuff in.

I have family who've spent time in prison, and to me, this sounds *very* much like being locked up, by choice. 'I think it's far worse than most prisons in a lot of ways, but you adapt. And the military is very good at keeping you busy,' he laughs. For those ten weeks it was doable, he says. But there were longer stints in the future alongside a spanner in the works: falling in love, and finally creating a home of his own.

Before all that, he was getting accustomed to his new family in the military. The nature of the work, and of the compact living environment meant that they easily developed a closeness, and quickly. At Dartmouth they were divided into divisions, each housing thirty of them: 'You absolutely generate some really good friendships, and that's one of the things that's most important about all of it – you're in it together.'

He talks very nonchalantly about his posting on ships like HMS *Ocean*. He spent six months at sea in the Mediterranean to oversee NATO operations in Libya. By this point though, he'd reached the high life and was able to share a six-man room, as opposed to thirty. 'It was bit nicer – nicer food, and everything else. You're treated more like adults.' As he talks it's all very matter of fact about the process, which I do understand. For him, this was his daily life. But for me, a civilian, it's a glimpse into a home life that was different to mine in every single way. He was living a life with different rules to the rest of us, but for him it was the adventure he'd always wanted.

And then he fell in love, during a very brief period working for the Ministry of Defence in London. But not long afterwards he was back to flying training, at places like RAF Cranwell in Lincolnshire and RAF Shawbury in Shropshire. As much as he enjoyed his training, the dynamics in his life had changed. He was embarking on a relationship that was beginning to mean a lot to him. As he talks, he explains that it felt like he was finally starting to set down roots with someone, in the midst of also doing the job he loved which would yank him away from those roots. Living the two lives was exhausting. 'Every weekend I'd be commuting back to London. When I was single it would be every now and then, and some weekends there were other young officers to go out with. But once I met Polly, I ended up having to find ways of commuting home more often.'

What James doesn't realise is that this is the first time that he's referred to *anywhere* as 'home'. Before this point he's referred to his parent's home, or just talked about living in a particular place, or a particular kind of accommodation. But has never referred to it as *his* home: it's clear at this point that the roots were starting to take hold, and create a foundation he'd never experienced before.

He spent a lot of time on the road in order to hang out with Polly; he'd leave the base on a Friday afternoon to drive down to London, spend Friday evening and Saturday together – then by Sunday late afternoon he'd be packed up and heading back up to Shropshire. As I talk to James I get the impression that Polly herself started to feel like home for him, a constant in a life that involved endless change and movement. Which he enjoyed, but when there is so much change in your life there tends to be a part of you that needs an anchor of sorts that makes at least one part of your life relatively calm. The couple then bought a house in London together and he finally set down proper, structural roots in 2014. A move that co-incided with a work assignment to RNAS (Royal Naval Air Station) Yeovilton in Somerset, meaning the Sunday night commute shifted to first thing on a Monday morning, so that the couple could enjoy their home together for an extra night.

Then James would leave and go to his Yeovilton accommodation. 'I definitely had two bedrooms. One that I shared with Polly in London, the other just for me in Yeovilton.'

Unlike the perfectly decorated home he shared with Polly, his accommodation at RNAS Yeovilton almost felt like he was 'regressing into childhood because you sort of make a little den that you close the door on and shut the rest of the military life out, for however many hours that you just needed to be alone.' He'd have his iPad for company so that he could watch movies to while away the hours of solitude. It was like living a double life.

But the longer stints away began as he was putting down roots with the love of his life. The joy of setting up home together was dampened by the continuous back and forth to base, and extended periods apart. By 2016 he was doing three to four months at a time. The conundrum was that he was finally doing the job that he loved, spending time in the skies. But the first love was taking him away from the love that replaced it. *She* was waiting for him at their home.

The following year brought the birth of their daughter, and all the joy that follows, including the family joining him in the marriage patch on the base for a while, which is the housing designated for the married partners of servicemen and women. Then he left for six months, leaving Polly to look after their daughter alone with the aid of grandparents and friends. It was a difficult time, he admits: 'It just became increasingly hard; I'd phone home and I'd realise that Polly obviously had a very stressful job in her own right, but then had to act as a single parent. While I'm here travelling around the world – yes, in a lot of ways having fun, and also doing something worthwhile, but ...' he pauses, 'at times, you're like, "I just want to be at home."'

He was deployed in 2020 too, during the Covid pandemic, leaving Polly alone with a young child, and isolated. 'There were times where I would feel totally hopeless when something would happen at home. Fundamentally, in the scheme of things it would be something random that would leave Polly totally stressed, like one of them would be ill. But Polly's parents were in Newcastle, and mine in Rutland, so none of them were round the corner to help out.'

Our children are roughly the same age, and I remember key moments when I'd be struggling with Alfie and at my wits' end with a combination of exhaustion and the constant, relentless cycle of parenting. I'd have some dark days at home, when dragging myself out of bed to the sound of Alfie's screams for another feed would have me on an emotional edge. But I was lucky enough to have my partner with me to help manage situations and give me a couple of hours break during the day to just ... breathe. James's support for Polly *was* there, but it was mostly only through audio and texts, not physically.

The nature of his job and the environment in which he was living meant that he had to be strict with the length of phone calls. He remembers times when he definitely had to get off the phone too early, leaving a situation unresolved, and then go fly a helicopter. It was the last thing he wanted to do at that very moment in time. Polly took the brunt of everything at home. It wasn't easy for either of them.

In his life's plan for being a helicopter pilot, he hadn't quite anticipated the pull of home. His life prior to falling in love had involved so much toing and froing, there hadn't been a thread that could yank at his heart with a need to be home. But I don't think any of us ever really understands the impact having kids can have on you. 'You're part of a family, but fundamentally not part of that family. It's such a horrible feeling,' he remembers. Though nothing could match the horrible feeling of finally coming home, but having been away for so long that your baby daughter has no idea who you are. 'Why would she know me? I'd been away for five months and was a stranger to her.' My heart aches for the emotional roller coaster the family were having to deal with at home.

And there was even more adjustment to come. Though the yearning for home and been satiated, he had to figure out how the three of them could live together effectively. Polly had developed a routine that worked for her life as a single parent: 'I had to figure where I fitted in this home, and how I fitted into this life again.'

You can imagine, can't you, two lives which had been so in sync when they first met, and so looking forward to deepening that connection when they created a home, only for that synchronisation to keep misfiring the longer they were kept apart. It must have, at times, been heartbreaking, especially for the man for whom setting down roots and creating a space that would feel like home seemed so out of reach in years gone by. As for Polly, when they first met, James *wasn't* spending long stints abroad, which was why their courtship was so much less complicated at the start. He'd be in her home every weekend whiling away the hours, doing very little in the way that only those in the first flushes of love can, as they get to know each other and create bonds.

If James had been disappearing for months during that

stage of their relationship, who knows where it would have headed. Instead, they were able to build the foundations of a home, which could withstand the constant batterings of distance. Perhaps it's because of the time spent building those foundations that James felt the place they currently live, very naturally, to be the only place he would refer to as home throughout our entire conversation, something which I'm not sure even he realised he did.

In that vein, perhaps it's also why his little dens on various ships began to resemble a space occupied not by a single man, but a father and husband living away from home, with more photographs and items which reminded him of home. 'You're used to getting to your cabin and putting your photos up everywhere, but when B came around and became a bit older, she started giving me soft toys. First it was an elephant, then I got a little spider.' She'd swap them round when she missed one of them, giving her dad the other to take with him to remind him of her. As if he could ever forget.

You can imagine, can't you, those moments where miscommunication at the end of a phone call make things seem so much worse. Rather than being able to hug out frustration with Polly, James could only send a text, stare at the pictures of his family on the walls of his den, and hold the soft animal given to him by his daughter. They were, he says, at breaking point. Something had to change.

The camaraderie on the ship helped though, because so many of the men and women around him were in exactly the same situation. Trying to manage a home life with life on a ship, he says, 'You'd sit around or do some exercise and someone afterwards would be like, oh I'm struggling because of whatever. And you'd be like, I'm struggling because of whatever. You'd sit and talk to people a bit more, especially during Covid. It wasn't a full-on therapy session, but it was a useful coping mechanism. You'd realise you weren't the only one.'

Strength in numbers is possibly what got them all through some really dark times aboard ship. That feeling of helplessness was always sat in the pit of his stomach: 'Something would happen at home and Polly would unload on me, and I'd sit there not able to do anything. I couldn't say I'd come home that evening and sort it out.' He says most of the scenarios would probably have been nothing if they had been living together. Which is, I guess, what made it hurt even more.

It could really only go in one direction. The thing that James loved so much in his life – taking to the skies in helicopters for the British military – had been superseded by the love of his wife, their daughter and their home. And although it was *technically* a choice, it really wasn't. He needed to be at home, the place that he could finally think of as a home, and set down those roots properly.

As a result, for James there's less flying and more teaching at a base on England's south coast, meaning less commuting, and more time spent at home, and more time learning what it means to be spending time at home. He's realised it's the place where he can really be himself: 'If I want to get up in my boxer shorts and go and make coffee, I can. No one's going to judge me. Whereas when you wake up on a ship you've got to get showered and changed, have a shave, sort your life out, *then* make a coffee.'

He continues, remembering life in his little den aboard the

ships that housed him over the years. 'You can make it your little man cave, and you can make it really comfortable. But it's never home. It's a place to get away from everything. It's a place to hide.' Whereas now, there is nothing to get away from. He's ensconced at home, slowly but surely becoming part of the furniture, and enjoying, finally, building relationships in the local area. Their doors open frequently to entertain visitors and cook beautiful meals.

'I think it's becoming a physical space. I think I've started feeling really relaxed in our house, more so than I ever have before. I can definitely go to my mum's house and feel this sort of regression into childhood of like, I'm at my mum's house now and my mum will just deal with it. Probably not what a thirty-eight-year-old man should be saying, but anyway, there's definitely a feeling of relaxation in my mother's house. But I can be myself in my home – you've got your home comforts, and it just feels homely.' A large part of that, he says, is because Polly and B are there.

Chapter 7

Serving the Motherland

My dad was already living in the UK when he decided to join the RAF, but over the years millions of people from the Commonwealth have joined the British Armed Forces in order to serve the 'motherland'. The contribution they have made to the safety of the UK isn't often heralded as much as it should be. Over 3 million soldiers and labourers from across the Commonwealth served alongside the British Army in the First World War, so it's not exactly a super recent development in world affairs.

As I've mentioned before, things weren't great at home when my dad decided to join the RAF. It was a form of escape, of sorts. He hadn't been in the country long when the armed forces became a feature in his life, and one could well imagine that being in the military environment in a new country would bring a level of homesickness – not for his new family home in London, but his life in Jamaica. But on arrival at the base after basic training, he was faced with groups of people who looked like him: those who had joined from Commonwealth countries.

Britain has always had a difficult relationship with its Commonwealth recruits, who have historically not been given the same rights as those who serve and are UK-born. This, despite the fact they too have made the decision to potentially sacrifice their lives for the good of the country. The imbalance has been highlighted time and time again. Just a couple of years ago, a UK inquiry blamed what they called 'pervasive racism' for the unequal commemoration of troops who died fighting for the Empire during the First World War. Up to 350,000 casualties, predominantly from Africa and the Middle East, may not be commemorated by name, or at all. The investigation found that up to 54,000 African and Asian casualties were commemorated 'unequally'. All those who die during the course of serving for their country are supposed to have their name engraved on a headstone over an identified grave or on a memorial to the missing. But not those whose skin was of a darker hue. Inequality existed even if you had *literally* laid down your life for a country who consistently rejected you.

The prevalence of this inequality was evident not that long ago, when the UK's government decided to waive the visa fees for those foreign and Commonwealth personnel who had completed six years in the forces or sustained injury. When I say not that long ago, we're only talking about 2022. Before then, after choosing to leave their homeland and give years of loyal service to the United Kingdom in the armed forces, they would still have to pay for the privilege to apply for indefinite leave to remain in the UK after their service ended. The then-Defence Secretary Ben Wallace said it was 'only right we have taken this important step to express our sincere gratitude'.[1]

It's a shame that it had taken so long really. But the payment still applies for the family that they left behind. They may have given loyal service, but that doesn't mean that their new home will welcome their families with open arms; their visa fee still applies.

But this doesn't dissuade those who choose to sign up to serve in the British Armed Forces, like David Vitalis, who made the decision to join the Army and leave the only home he knew in St Lucia. It's an island that's mostly covered in lush rainforest, and known for the Pitons mountain range, and, like so many Caribbean islands, for its plethora of distilleries turning sugar cane into rum. They speak St Lucian Creole. Creole is a local language formed by mostly African enslaved people shaped by contact with a European language, especially English, French, Spanish or Portuguese. Due to its colonial roots, the St Lucia version is based on French.

David saw an advert, as part of a big recruitment drive by the Army, to encourage those in the Commonwealth to think about joining up and serving the country which used to be its colonial master. For David, it was a chance to see the world. 'I've always had *pat cho*, which is hot feet. I always wanted to travel all over the world and move around and stuff.'

(*Pat cho* translation: someone who refuses to stay at home and is always on the move is said to have *pat cho*.)

In terms of the move itself, he harboured no feelings of fear. 'I had mixed emotions: I was excited, I wasn't scared. It was the chance for a new beginning, to start afresh.' The week before intake he took the opportunity to party as much as he could, almost like getting it all out of his system before his life changed for ever. The magnitude of the situation wasn't lost on him, or the daunting task ahead – so he decided to make the most of his final few days of freedom and get to know his new home in possibly the best way a young person can: he partied. He laughs as he thinks back to that time. 'I went clubbing every single night. And it was funny because when I got on the train to the base, I was drunk, because I'd come straight from a nightclub.'

But interspersed in all of the joy of being somewhere new and the adventures that lay ahead, he was sad to leave his home, to leave his family. 'If someone were to fall ill or die, I wouldn't have the luxury of just jumping in a car and going to them.' He was acutely aware of just how far away he was from the life he was leaving behind, especially his mum. 'I was worried about what I'd do if the inevitable happened, and when I would be able to say goodbye.'

It was his mother's home that he knew he'd miss the most when he made that journey, and the smells of her cooking up a storm in their kitchen. Most specifically, a dish called bouillon. To look at, it's not dissimilar to a Jamaican red pea soup that I was raised on at home. Bouillon is a one-pot dish which contains dried beans or peas, vegetables and flour dumplings, and can also contain meat. As with many traditional dishes, the exact specifics of the dish can vary between families. And like so many countries who were colonized, the dish has aspects of the colonisers – in this instance, France and Britain. It also has aspects of African and Indian cultures too, such is the nature of its history within the slave trade and servitude. The French influences of the dish are apparent from the name alone, bouillon, which means broth in English and comes from the word '*bouillir*' which means to boil. It's a meal that is reflective of its history, like so many dishes created out of various experiences of colonialism across the Caribbean.

Like so many countries in the Caribbean that endured the centuries of the slave trade, the meal was invented by those who had very little but needed to create meals that would sustain them for a day's work as an enslaved person. The African enslaved people and their indentured servant counterparts who hailed from India created it out of cheap cuts of meat that their slave masters had little interest in eating. In this case pigtails, snouts, chicken feet, trotters, etc. There are many key meals in Jamaica which also use very similar cuts of meats in its recipes, for exactly the same reason (pig foot brown stew is one).

The meats were preserved, and the herbs and spices added to up the stakes flavour-wise. Then, much like in Jamaican red pea soup, things like yam, cassava, and chocho were added. Although in St Lucia cassava and chocho are known as yuca and tannia respectively. When all of that is combined you get a dish that produces the smells and history of St Lucia.

But on that journey to the UK, it simply wasn't practical or possible for David to pack a pot of bouillon in his suitcase. The answer, considering his exploits when he first arrived in the country, will possibly come as no surprise: 'Bounty Rum.' Stuffed between his clothes and toiletries he'd packed three bottles of rum, which I'm sure went down a treat with the other recruits when he arrived at base. 'You cannot go wrong with Bounty Rum – you speak to any St Lucian and they will tell you.' I'll take his word for it. As a Jamaican, the only rum that passes my lips is Appleton, and as far as I'm concerned it's the most superior rum in the Caribbean. For the uninitiated, every Caribbean island that produces rum believes that *they* have the most superior rum in the region. But to be honest, there's just no competition when it comes to Appleton, so the others really should fall back and take their place behind the clear winner.

Anyway, I digress.

Thankfully it wasn't just rum that filled his case, in terms of memories of home. He packed photos of his family, a necklace, and a silver ring that his mum made him. However, as much as he wanted to keep it on at all times as a reminder of home, and of his mum, he wasn't allowed. So he started a routine of taking the ring off when he was in uniform, and putting it back on when he was in civilian clothes. But the inevitable happened: 'One day it fell out of my pocket and one of the trucks passed over it, and it got disfigured. And that was the end of that.'

He left a lot back in St Lucia – there was no need to take everything – but the one thing he regrets *not* taking is his beloved coin collection. Especially a very rare one that his mum spent one day when she needed loose change. Retelling this part of the story, you get the sense that David hasn't ever really forgiven her for that.

The Pirbright Army Training Centre was the first place he ended up in his new home country. It's about thirty miles west of London, in Woking. There, they do the initial fourteen-week training course that's compulsory for all new recruits when they join the Army. For some, the reality of the task ahead could seem overwhelming, but upon entering the facility David noticed several other recruits from the Commonwealth, and it helped to settle any nerves that he may have had. 'Some of us were from St Lucia, others from St Vincent, another guy was from Trinidad, and we all stayed together.'

I've mentioned before about the comfortableness that comes from being alongside those with a shared experience. And I can imagine that when you are thousands of miles away from home, and serving in an Army in which you are a minority, there is a certain amount of strength that can be gleaned from knowing that you're *not the only one*. (Just as an aside, as of April 2022, ethnic minorities represented 2.8% of officers and 11.2% of other ranks in the regular forces.[2])

Their living accommodation was as basic as you would imagine. As he describes it, it was just a room with a normal bed and a table. But those first few weeks sound genuinely fascinating in terms of how the men were encouraged to work as one in their new home, presumably to create a family-like atmosphere early on. They would need close relationships for the work which was to come. 'If we wanted to do anything, we would all have to move together. Nobody could move by themselves. We had to move in pairs or as a single unit: if you wanted to watch television we had to go down together. So if one person wanted to go, they had to hope someone else wanted to go too. You had to walk in step with each other.' The way in which the Army creates discipline and teamwork really is very interesting.

The system of hierarchy at home begins early in the Army in terms of who lives where, why, and with how many. 'You had a differentiation. If you lived in our block, the old block, that was like the ghetto section of Pirbright. And then you had the bourgeois section up the hill.' I definitely have never heard Army accommodation called 'bourgeois' before, and it tickles me.

His eyes were only opened to the variation in facilities

when he first became ill with chicken pox, an outbreak that took all the Commonwealth guys down. Not a single one of them had been exposed to it as a child, so their immune system at that point was very different to those recruits who were UK-born. 'When you get injured you get moved, and I was injured, I had chicken pox – so they moved us.' When they arrived they realised this new bourgeois block had a television within the block and better toilets. It was a whole new world. He laughs when he remembers. (What's wonderful about talking with David is what joy he clearly got from being in the Army environment, despite the horrors of war, death and destruction that he would witness in the later years.)

As fun an environment as it was, it was never homely, he says, especially when the Army was moving towards bigger bases. The impact of the bigger bases, apart from more personnel and more modern amenities, meant a slightly different dining experience, much to his disappointment. Mass-produced English food was simply not his cup of tea. 'Every Sunday for us in the Caribbean you have your proper meal. You have your coleslaw, your red bean soup, your rice and peas, your big chicken stew. You know, there's a whole selection. But an Army Sunday roast?' He sighs. 'You just look at it and think, "Why is it so bland? What's up with that?!"'

It's safe to say that his culinary tastes, finely tuned after years of a Caribbean diet at home, were not being fulfilled in an Army canteen in Catterick. But he says there would be rays of hope if they got a chef with a love of cooking. 'You could actually taste that this person had really put some effort into it. But then, when you're eating rice and it's still hard, that says a lot about what the chef thinks about food.

Especially when the custard is so runny you think, "Should I just drink this with a straw?"'

The variations in quality, and the yearning for food from home that he was raised on, pushed him to buy a two-hob stove and just do it himself. 'I started cooking my own food when I got to Yorkshire. So on a Sunday I would do a big chicken, stew fish, macaroni and cheese. I just said, 'Do you know what, enough is enough.' I was going to have a feast on a Sunday. I wanted to eat my own food.'

He then started a routine which would mean consuming as little of the bland English food as possible, and more of his own home-cooked meals. He'd cook huge pots of food on a Sunday night which would last him till Thursday. Then he'd travel to his aunt's in south-east London on a Friday afternoon, eat *her* Caribbean feast, then head back to cook his own on the Sunday evening. It was a laborious routine, but one that made him, and his belly, very happy.

But the nature of serving in the Army means not every base was in the UK, and not every environment warranted a full St Lucian feast. His job took him to places like Germany, Kenya, Bosnia, Iraq, Afghanistan, Kuwait, Canada, Croatia, Poland and the Czech Republic.

When you're stationed at bases abroad, things are different. It's not a home away from home, it's the furthest thing from it. The instinct is to bring things from home to remind you of what you've left behind, so that you feel less isolated. And to remind you of whatever you witness during the horrors of war, you are loved at home:

'You'd have what we call a comfy box where you would keep all your memorabilia and stuff. My first couple of tours were around the second Iraq War, and I packed a comfy box of things like photographs, loads of books, DVD box sets' – his box sets of choice were *Star Trek* – 'and a comfy feather pillow. But then you move up the ranks and you realise all you need is your laptop; you don't need all the pictures.'

It was after his first couple of tours that one of his sergeants suggested that he didn't pack a comfy box at all. He didn't understand why at first, but it became clearer the longer he did tours for. 'The less stuff you go up with [on tour], the less they have to pack when you don't make it back.'

This hit me like a juggernaut. Among all our banter up until this point, it had never crossed my mind that if you don't survive your tour, it is your friends that will have to pack everything up. Each item they would hold in their hand to pack meant something special to their friend, it would make them feel closer to home when so far away. But it would also serve as a reminder to *them* that the loss was so much bigger than their unit, and, of course, a reminder of their own mortality. 'I remember when we were in Afghanistan and we had to repatriate some of the guys' stuff. Packing up your friend's stuff. If you're packing their military kit, it's emotional. But it's more emotional when you start packing up the personal kit.'

Choosing not to take that personal kit with you is quite the sacrifice on behalf of the squadron that you serve alongside: leaving behind pictures and items of sentimental value during possibly one of the scariest, most high-pressured and traumatic environments you could ever find yourself in. It's quite something. Instead, you rely on phone calls for that connection. He said those Paradigm minutes (thirty minutes of government-funded phone calls to any military personnel deployed on two to six month tours) meant the world to him. The lack of visual connection to the home that he'd left behind meant that being able to hear the voice of home, the voice of his mother, took on even more significance.

Despite the loss, the trauma, and the pressurised environment, David enjoyed being on tour. 'I looked forward to it,' he says. 'Yes, in places like Iraq and Afghanistan there was the danger element to it, but because of my squadron I had people that I always looked forward to working with.'

He tells me a story of working alongside a guy named Tucker in Iraq. As they waited for a ride, Tucker came up to him and asked if he had a housewife. Confused, David said, 'No, I've never been married, what are you talking about?' 'No. No. No. A housewife,' Tucker replied. Again, David repeated that he wasn't married. Suddenly the alarm went off and rockets started being fired at them, so everyone scrambled to the floor with their helmets and body armour on, covering their heads.

'And this dude Tucker comes up to me and says, "Do you have a needle and thread?"' David is cracking up at this point of the story. It turns out that a 'housewife kit' is a pouch carried by soldiers to carry the sewing/repair kits they're provided with. 'So I was like, "Tucker, we're getting rocketed." And he replied, "Exactly. I don't want to die holding my pants [trousers]."'

He says conversations like that are why, when people ask him if he misses the Army, he says no. It's the people he misses, the camaraderie and the jokes that they shared. 'When it came to deploying you could rest assured that when the shit hit the fan, you knew you were gonna put your life on the line to save them.' There's such power and peace that comes with that.

Having now left the Army and living at home in Surrey full-time with his wife and two young children, it's been an adjustment – as with James, he's learning to settle into the place that he now calls home. But it's twofold for David. He's adjusting to living now as a *civilian* in the UK, having only ever lived in it as a soldier, and is also getting used to being with his family without going back to the military at regular intervals. 'It's a totally different dynamic,' he says. But one which he is enjoying.

Much like my dad, David was convinced that once he finished in the Army he would return back to St Lucia, leaving the cold and grey of London behind. He had no intention of applying for his UK visa, and had little interest in a British passport. Despite serving several tours in some of the most dangerous areas on the world on behalf of Britain, the plan wasn't necessarily to go all in and make this his home. But it was his captain in Germany who insisted that it was the right thing to do, especially since he had laid his life on the line for the country.

Shocked that it hadn't crossed David's mind, the captain wasted no time in getting the ball rolling. He got the documents together that David needed for his application, and wrote his supporting letter the very next day, a move that David is thankful for. It's interesting, isn't it? One would assume that he would see it as what he deserves after what he'd put himself through on behalf of the British Army, but he didn't feel as though it owed him anything. He was thankful for the Army experience, and happy to do it.

But once he left the Army, he realised that having been away from St Lucia for twenty-one years – his was a career that involved tours of some of the most dangerous places in the world, as well as UK based roles – he now feels like a foreigner when he returns to visit. It just doesn't feel the same, so much so that when he travels to St Lucia now with his family, they choose to stay in hotels, rather than at his mum's house. Time and changing circumstance means that the place that was home for the first stage of his life, is no longer the place he calls home. Despite this, though, he says it will always *feel* like home. 'It's more, I think, my sense of pride in terms of where I am from.'

In two decades, his mindset has changed, something which he wasn't expecting. But it's a change that makes him happy and settled, fully adjusted to the new way of living. It's now his home in the UK that he thinks of when he thinks of the concept of home, he says. 'My family, my kids, my wife. For me, that is home.'

Conclusion

Through the process of speaking to contributors for this book, and from speaking to family and friends about what home means to them, it's fairly obvious that there are some central themes regarding the concept of 'home': a place of safety, a place of family, a place that you hold delicately in your heart. And yet everybody has a slightly different version of what they see as home and why, and there is such beauty in that. No two stories are the same. There is no wrong answer.

The place that we see as home is the hook that an invisible thread can tie itself to, the other end of which moulds itself into something that suctions onto our hearts, forever a part of who we are.

No matter where we are in the world, no matter where we are mentally or emotionally, that invisible thread is possibly the strongest of all threads. It manages to tug at our hearts both in moments of joy and sadness. Even if it's connected to a feeling rather than a physical place, it can tug all the same. So much of who we are, and who we go on to become, is inextricably linked to that invisible thread that so delicately follows us through our path in life.

But it can be more than one place and be more than one thing.

The thread that hooks onto my heart splits like a fork in the road . . . one end leads to England, the other to the Jamaican culture in which I was raised. Sometimes the tug of one is stronger than the other, but that's okay because that too is a reflection of me. I can be more English than Jamaican at times, and vice versa. But that doesn't make me any less British-Jamaican, not at all. It is possible for my heart to belong to two 'homes'; it's big enough to cope. So why should I feel like I have to choose one? My heart feels safe being attached to two homes, and I gain a lot of joy from being a part of two places. It's empowering.

Feeling safe, and the idea of safety, is an obvious part of how we feel about the place we call home. But it's important that we don't forget that feeling safe in your home is a privilege. The children's home that Chris was sent to wasn't safe so he had to run away, Yuliia and Alex's home in Ukraine wasn't safe so they had to flee, Leyli's dad can't bring his family to the home he holds so dear in his heart because it's not the 'home' he left so many years ago. The history of how we see our homes also tells the history of how we see ourselves, and in turn that is a reflection of the social history of the world – and of how the homes of some are seen as more important than the homes of others.

The UN sees housing and a home as the 'basis of stability and security for an individual or family.' They go on to say, '[It is] the centre of our social, emotional and sometimes economic lives. A home should be a sanctuary – a place to live in peace, security and dignity.'[1]

No matter where you identify your home to be, whether it is physical or emotional, it essentially boils down to exactly that. But the reality of life is that in the history of the displaced, there are so many like Chris who spend years trying to find a physical space they can call home. There are those who yearn for the safety of the home again, but spend years unable to grab hold of it and hold it tight. Instead, they can spend their entire lives with it just outside their grasp. Each time they reach for it, it moves slight further away: a dream unfulfilled. The UN sees housing as a human right, but perhaps we should also be looking at the idea of 'home' also being a human right: four walls may equal a house, but it doesn't mean it's a home that's safe.

The memories of our home dim over time. We don't remember every story, we don't remember every meal ... but we do know how it made us feel. Every day in my home growing up wasn't a bed of roses or a road paved with gold, of course not. But it's the moments that made me feel loved, the moments that made me feel wanted, the moments that brought me joy and security: those are the bits that shine brightly in my memory. And it's that feeling that we hold in our hearts every single day. When you are afforded the luxury of stability and a good home life, it plays so much into the adults we become.

But the question of home and identity are so tightly interwoven for those from immigrant communities. The need to not forget the roots from which you came is strong; it's so powerful and necessary in order to navigate a country in which you are a minority. My dad has never forgotten where he is from, and missed being immersed in it for most of his life: the joy that he felt when he moved back was unparalleled. However, when he's there he misses his home in London, and vice versa. His heart, too, is split like a fork in the road. He, too, belongs to both.

But then you add on the experiences of Leyli's dad, and Alex and Yuliia, and their memories of home – and what it used to be – are fixed in the past. Always yearning for a home which in their absence has changed so much over time, their memories of home only exist in the past. How that home made them feel is frozen in a time that no longer exists, suspended in a reality that lives on in their minds and their memories. And the only way to share that feeling, to share *why* they feel the way they do, is by sharing their stories. That way, even if the physical reality of their home has changed, sometimes irreparably, the reason *why* it fills their hearts never does. And sharing that reality makes it feel real again, and ensures those memories are not lost for ever. Their home, though lost to war or revolution, remains cemented in the hearts of those they love the most.

But in terms of how I feel about that combination of British and Jamaican ... what Yue'er said about the blood flowing through her children's veins rings true to me. The blood in me is 100 per cent Jamaican. I mean, yes, it's technically West African, but my connection to my history only goes as far back as the Caribbean, so it's the place I feel most drawn to in my ancestry. I'm proud of my blood being 100 per cent Jamaican, and I'm proud that my children also share my Jamaican DNA. A part of them, too, hails from elsewhere. And I'd love for them to also feel Jamaica in their heart as they grow older.

Legally I am British and my home is here, but my blood is Jamaican so my home is also there. They are both part of who I am. The British part of me wouldn't exist had my family not decided to take that leap out of enslavement to begin again, and generations later decided to take a different kind of leap and set up home thousands of miles away in Britain. And that's why I had that reaction at the top of the hill in Clarendon – a decision made then was the catalyst to new 'homes' being created and new opportunities being grabbed. And I think it was the realisation that that small patch of land was the home where it all began, which just felt crazy to me. And yet, also necessary in the understanding of myself and the whole essence of 'returning home'. It was as though I was returning to my ancestors to reassure them that yes, their sacrifice worked out in the way they had hoped, and their souls could rest easy with the knowledge that the physical pain, the sacrifice, the loss and the hurt *did* eventually end.

Claude McKay's final words in the poem 'I Shall Return' are: 'I shall return again, to ease my mind of long, long years of pain.' Where is the place that you return to, to ease your pain? Where is home in your heart?

The pride I feel in my family for making the decision to help Britain rebuild while also improving themselves economically is immense.

We are all drawn to different places according to how we view 'home' and there is such beauty in that; it shows how much of where we come from is in our hearts. And it can be more difficult to explain a feeling or a smell rather than a physical structure or place, but that's okay. I still can't fully explain my reaction at the top of that hill in Clarendon, Jamaica, but I suppose I can put it down to pride. Pride, and an understanding that the decisions we make in our homes and our lives will continue to have repercussions for generations to come, and that when we set down our roots in those homes the impact will be felt for ever. It's a powerful way to look at life, and perhaps gives us the understanding that though we are here for a short time, the footsteps we tentatively take in the present will never be forgotten.

Notes

Introduction

1. Office for National Statistics, 'Regional ethnic diversity' (22 December 2022), www.ethnicity-facts-figures.service.gov.uk/uk-population-by-ethnicity/national-and-regional-populations/regional-ethnic-diversity/latest, accessed 26 November 2023
2. Wilmot, Swithin, 'Free Villages', Encyclopedia.com (2005), www.encyclopedia.com/history/encyclopedias-almanacs-transcripts-and-maps/free-villages, accessed 26 November 2023

Chapter 1

1. www.bl.uk/windrush/articles/how-caribbean-migrants-rebuilt-britain
2. 'Empire Windrush: Life for Migrants in the 1940s and 50s', The National Archives, www.nationalarchives.gov.uk/education/resources/the-empire-windrush/empire-windrush-life-for-migrants-in-the-1940s-and-50s/#:~:text=Finding%20accommodation%20became%20difficult%20for,teddy%20boys'%20and%20new%20arrivals, accessed 26 November 2023
3. Olofinjana, Israel Oluwole, 'The History of Black Majority Churches in London', The Open University (2010), www5.open.ac.uk/arts/research/religion-in-london/resource-guides/black-majority-church#:~:text=The%201940s%20and%201950s%20saw,Caribbean%20Pentecostal%20and%20Holiness%20Churches, accessed 26 November 2023
4. Theo's Think Tank, www.theosthinktank.co.uk, accessed 26 November 2023
5. 'Why don't hair salons want Black money', GalDem (16 June 2018) gal-dem.com/hair-salons-black-money/, accessed 26 November 2023
6. White, Shane and White, Graham, 'Slave Hair and African American Culture in the Eighteenth and Nineteenth Centuries', The Journal of Southern History, Vol. 61, No 1 (February 1995), pp. 45–76, www.thefreelibrary.com/Slave+clothing+and+African-American+culture+in+the+eighteenth+and...-a017474755, accessed 26 November 2023

7. '6 Things Everyone Should Know About Black Hair History', Odele (22 February 2021), odelebeauty.com/blogs/the-rinse/black-hair-history-facts#:~:text=One%20of%20the%20first%20things,their%20connection%20to%20their%20cultures, accessed 26 November 2023

8. Gillborn, David, 'Ethnicity and Educational Performance in the United Kingdom: Racism, Ethnicity, and Variability in Achievement', *Anthropology & Education Quarterly*, Vol. 28, No. 3 (September 1997), www.researchgate.net/profile/David-Gillborn/publication/227752990_Ethnicity_and_Educational_Performance_in_the_United_Kingdom_Racism_Ethnicity_and_Variability_in_Achievement/links/59ad9d51a6fdcce55a416802/Ethnicity-and-Educational-Performance-in-the-United-Kingdom-Racism-Ethnicity-and-Variability-in-Achievement.pdf, accessed 26 November 2023

9. 'Black and Ethnic Minority Young People and Educational Disadvantage', Runnymede Trust (September 1997), assets-global.website-files.com/61488f992b58e687f1108c7c/617bff72c25e78868e678415_BMEYoungPeopleandEducationalDisadvantage-97.PDF, accessed 19 December 2023

10. 'Racial Equality in Prisons: A formal investigation by the Commission for Racial Equality into HM Prison Service of England and Wales', Commission for Racial Equality (December 2003), image.guardian.co.uk/sys-files/Society/documents/2003/12/16/CREPrisons.pdf, accessed 26 November 2023

11. Audini, Bernard and Lelliot, Paul, 'Age, gender and ethnicity of those detained under Part II of the Mental Health Act 1983', *British Journal of Psychiatry*, Vol. 180, issue 3 (March 2002), pp. 222–226, web.archive.org/web/20190502000506id_/https://www.cambridge.org/core/services/aop-cambridge-core/content/view/D3D2D14174B8880336A1E6CDE254AA17/S0007125000268207a.pdf/div-class-title-age-gender-and-ethnicity-of-those-detained-under-part-ii-of-the-mental-health-act-1983-div.pdf, accessed November 26 2023.

12. Martin Webster, speech, *South London Press* (5 August 1977).

13. 'Migration Histories', The National Archives (5 December 2013), webarchive.nationalarchives.gov.uk/ukgwa/+/http://www.movinghere.org.uk/galleries/histories/caribbean/growing_up/education.htm, accessed 26 November 2023

14. 'Disgraceful Labelling: Race, Special Education and Exclusion', Excluded Lives (14 July 2021), excludedlives.education.ox.ac.uk/disgraceful-labelling-race-special-education-and-exclusion, accessed 19 December 2023

Chapter 2

1. 'Uncovering The Past Abuse of Children in Care', The Care Leavers' Association, www.careleavers.com/history/#:~:text=During%20the%201990s%20and%20into,Ireland%2C%20Canada%20and%20Australia, accessed 26 November 2023

2. Wolmar, Christian, 'Forgotten Children – the background to the

children's homes scandals', *Independent on Sunday* (8 October 2000), www.christianwolmar.co.uk/2000/10/forgotten-children-the-background-to-the-childrens-homes-scandals/, accessed 26 November 2023

3. Kirkwood, Andrew, 'The Leicestershire Inquiry 1992', The Therapeutic Care Journal (1 December 2011), thetcj.org/child-care-history-policy/the-leicestershire-inquiry-1992-by-andrew-kirkwood, accessed 26 November 2023

4. Roberts, Yvonne, '"We were abused every day". Decades on, children's homes victims wait for justice', *Observer* (8 February 2020), www.theguardian.com/uk-news/2020/feb/08/care-home-victims-wait-for-justice-decades-on-institutional-child-abuse, accessed 26 November 2023

5. 'BRIEFING: Access to Housing for young women leaving care who are at risk from violence, abuse and exploitation', SaferLondon (April 2020), saferlondon.org.uk/wp-content/uploads/2020/04/SLbriefing youngwomenleavingcare.pdf, accessed 26 November 2023

Chapter 3

1. 'MV Empire Windrush (The New Zealand Shipping Company Ltd)', The National Archives, discovery.nationalarchives.gov.uk/details/r/C9152210, accessed 26 November 2023

2. Resolve, 'In the margins: the influence of the Caribbean diaspora', The Architectural Review (7 June 2019), www.architectural-review.com/essays/in-the-margins-the-influence-of-the-caribbean-diaspora, accessed 26 November 2023

3. Booth, Robert, 'Ethnic segregation in England and Wales on the wane, research finds', *The Guardian* (17 Jan 2023), www.theguardian.com/uk-news/2023/jan/17/ethnic-segregation-in-england-and-wales-on-the-wane-research-finds#:~:text=The%20places%20with%20the%20lowest,British%20in%20the%202021%20census, accessed 26 November 2023

4. Chu, Ben, 'Why are Chinese students so keen on the UK?', BBC News (5 March 2022), www.bbc.co.uk/news/uk-scotland-60587499, accessed 26 November 2023

5. Mingjie, Wang, 'Nation sends record number of students to UK', ChinaDaily.com (2 October 2023), global.chinadaily.com.cn/a/202302/10/WS63e59f6ca31057c47ebae064.html, accessed 26 November 2023

6. 'Hong Kong: Cultural life – cultural milieu and the arts', Britannica, www.britannica.com/place/Hong-Kong/Cultural-life, accessed 26 November 2023

7. Lu Kestell, Judy and Meinheit, Harold, 'Hong Kong: From Fishing Village to Financial Center', Library of Congress Information Bulletin (August 1997), www.loc.gov/loc/lcib/9708/hongkong.html, accessed 26 November 2023

8. British Library, www.bl.uk/learning/timeline/item107673.html

9. Ibid.

10. 'Beijing Cuisine – Flavors, Famous Dishes, Food Menu', Travel China Guide, www.travelchinaguide.com/beijing- cuisine.htm#:~:text= Origin%20%26%20Development%20of%20Beijing%20Cuisine& text=In%20the%207th%20century%2C%20Muslims,Beijing%20 and%20influenced%20each%20other, accessed 26 November 2023
11. 'Chinese Imperial Dishes – Imperial Cuisine', China.org.cn, www. china.org.cn/english/imperial/26125.htm, accessed 26 November 2023
12. 'Resolution on certain questions in the history of our party since the founding of the People's Republic of China', Marxists.org, www. marxists.org/subject/china/documents/cpc/history/01.htm, accessed 26 November 2023
13. Martin, Fran, 'Overseas study as 'escape route' for young Chinese women', University of Nottingham Asia Research Unit (22 June 2016), theasiadialogue.com/2016/06/22/single-and-mobile-overseas-study-as-escape-route-for-young-chinese-women/, accessed 26 November 2023

Chapter 4

1. 'Kosiv – guidebook', Shtetl Routes, shtetlroutes.eu/en/kosv-putvnik/, accessed 26 November 2023

Chapter 5

1. 'How Many Immigrants Are In The UK?', Immigration Advice Service, iasservices.org.uk/how- many- immigrants- are- in-theuk/#:~:text=As%20of%20the%20year%20ending,of%20the%20 total%20UK%20population, accessed 26 November 2023
2. 'Births by parents' country of birth, England and Wales: 2022', Office of National Statistics, www.ons.gov.uk/peoplepopulation andcommunity/birthsdeathsandmarriages/livebirths/bulletins/ parentscountryofbirthenglandandwales/2022#:~:text=5.,from%20 15.5%25%20in%202021), accessed 26 November 2023
3. 'Life in Iran before the 1979 Islamic Revolution', *The Week* (22 November 2022), theweek.com/news/society/958583/life-in-iran-before-the-1979-islamic-revolution, accessed 26 November 2023
4. Kazmir, Munr, 'Before and After: Iran 1979', International Policy Digest (22 February 2019), intpolicydigest.org/before-and-after-iran-1979/, accessed 26 November 2023
5. Priborkin, Emily, '40 Years Later: Iran after the Islamic Revolution', American University (8 April 2019), www.american.edu/sis/ news/20190408-40-years-later-iran-after-the-islamic-revolution. cfm#:~:text=Aftermath%20and%20Present%2DDay%20 Iran&text=Debates%2C%20liberties%2C%20and%20freedoms%20 that,were%20executed%20or%20held%20hostage, accessed 26 November 2023
6. Blackmore, Erin, 'This ancient festival is a celebration of springtime – and a brand new year', *National Geographic* (15 March 2022), www.nationalgeographic.com/history/article/nowruz-

ancient-festival-celebration-springtime-new-year#:~:text=Nowruz
%20has%20been%20celebrated%20in,as%20a%20victory%20
over%20darkness, accessed 26 November 2023

Chapter 7

1. 'Visa fees scrapped for Non-UK Service Personnel', UK government,
   (23 February 2022), https://www.gov.uk/government/news/visa-
   fees-scrapped-for-non-uk-service-personnel, accessed 1 May 2024
2. 'UK armed forces biannual diversity statistics: 1 April 2022', UK
   Government, www.gov.uk/government/statistics/uk-armed-forces-
   biannual-diversity-statistics-april-2022/uk-armed-forces-biannual-
   diversity-statistics-1-april-2022, accessed 22 December 2023

Conclusion

1. Special Rapporteur on Housing, 'The human right to adequate
   housing', United Nations – Office of the High Commissioner of
   Human Rights, www.ohchr.org/en/special-procedures/sr-housing/
   human-right-adequate-housing#:~:text=Increasingly%20viewed%20
   as%20a%20commodity,home%20or%20lands%20taken%20away,
   accessed 26 November 2023

Acknowledgements

This book is dedicated to the millions of families and children, both here and abroad, still searching for a safe place to call home.

Thank you to my mum, dad, grandparents, aunts and uncles for giving me and my siblings a safe place to live, full of love and opportunity. We are who we are because of you.

There aren't enough words to describe just how thankful I am to all the contributors to this book, who trusted me to tell their stories. The pseudonyms which are used in some parts are in place to ensure their safety and that of their families.

To my book agent Elise Middleton, gosh ... there's no way I would've even had the confidence to begin this journey without you. Your words of encouragement, and your patience with me, instilled a belief that I could actually pull this off – despite my many wobbles. Thank you to my YMU team Melanie Rockcliffe, Rebekka Taylor and Charly Briscombe for always standing by me. To my publisher Sharmaine Lovegrove, I'm still not convinced you truly understand what an inspiration you are to me and so many others. Babes, you're amazing. To have your guidance through this means the world to me. And to the wider Dialogue publishing team:

project editor Eleanor Gaffney, Tom Neilson from Midas PR and Emily Moran in marketing ... all of you have a hand in this story, so thank you so much for everything.

Thank you to the staff at my local Harris & Hoole coffee shop who've kept me company for months as I sat in there for hours drinking tea and writing. I'm thankful for the music that filled my mind through the headphones which were for ever clamped to my ears while writing there: the likes of Lil Simz, Beyoncé, Stormzy and Fleetwood Mac. And a heart-shaped thank you goes out to my former English teacher Mrs Broadbridge who sparked my love of storytelling.

And finally, this book is also dedicated to my partner Andy, and our children Florence and Alfie ... and our home which we want them to return to for ever.

Bringing a book from manuscript to what you are reading is a team effort.

Renegade Books would like to thank everyone who helped to publish *No Place Like Home* in the UK.

Editorial
Sharmaine Lovegrove
Joelle Owusu-Sekyere
Eleanor Gaffney

Contracts
Megan Phillips
Bryony Hall
Amy Patrick
Anne Goddard

Sales
Caitriona Row
Dominic Smith
Frances Doyle
Hannah Methuen
Lucy Hine
Toluwalope Ayo-Ajala

Design
Nico Taylor

Production
Narges Nojoumi

Publicity
Tom Neilson

Marketing
Emily Moran

Operations
Kellie Barnfield
Millie Gibson
Sameera Patel
Sanjeev Braich

Finance
Andrew Smith
Ellie Barry

Audio
Binita Naik

Copy-Editor
Saxon Bullock

Proofreader
Oliver Cotton